Grow Up

Growing Your Business & Yourself

Paige Weslaski

ISBN–13: 978–1727064223
ISBN–10: 1727064224

Paige Weslaski

To all the dreamers, big and small.

Paige Weslaski

'The plans of the diligent lead surely to abundance.'

~ Proverbs 21:5

Grow Up

Paige Weslaski

A Little Appetizer:

Your Last Day

"Everything that happens before Death is what counts." – Ray Bradbury

Walking up the steps of your neighborhood church, you take one final breath. Quietly un-hatching the door and inching it open, you hear the ceremony already in progress.

It's unlike you to sleep in and miss a service, especially after being told it's a special occasion, and you avoid the thought of your significant others' 'I told you not to be late!' yet again.

Flower bouquets neatly placed in the entryway and a handful of people milling in and out of the bathroom, you walk toward the sanctuary and enter.

A couple hundred people in attendance, your

family sitting front row with friends and acquaintances strewn throughout the back, you feel a sense of ease.

You know these people; you recognize their names, their stories, their lives. Some you know better than others, some you vaguely know from times past; but they all ignite at least a hint of remembrance in your mind.

Not wanting to disturb the service, you sneak toward a chair in the last row and take off your hat.

Clearing your throat, you smile and give a little wave to the old woman sitting next to you – the checkout clerk from the grocery store who weekly talks your ear off – and for whatever reason she looks the other way without so much as a head nod.

Ignoring her uncharacteristic rudeness, you fix your eyes on the empty pulpit and notice your best friend, of all people, walking toward it.

Confused, not recalling them mentioning being scheduled to speak, you pat yourself on the back for at least remembering to come. What a shame it would be to miss this!

Waiting expectantly for your best friend to begin, a smile of pride on your face, your smile fades ever so slowly. Not only did they start speaking in a dismal, low tone – very unlike them – but they looked grave as a stone. They weren't their peppy self. In fact, rather melancholy. Mournful, almost.

Confused, you listen closely to their words, trying to piece together reasoning for the dismal behavior. What had gotten into them on this beautiful, sunny day?

Hearing their words, you don't quite know what they mean. They begin to speak about you, of all people, explaining how you had an impact on their life.

Wondering where on earth they were going with this and what they were bringing you up for, your heart grows cold with their next words.

"I never thought losing my best friend would be this difficult, yet I..."

With that, your throat closes tightly and your hands begin to shake. Your eyes well up and your breathe grows deep and quick. You try standing to your feet, but find them glued to the floor.

As the room seems to move, you — although feeling confused and dizzy — stand and drag yourself to the next row.

Hobbling your feet one foot in front of the other, you spot your neighbor, a kind, young fella, and kneel beside him.

"Um, what is this?" you whisper, a feeling of confusion and dread in your mind.

Without even turning his head, he continues to look toward your friend.

Giving your neighbor a strong nudge, you ask again. "What is this?," more demanding than you planned.

Same as before, reaction–less.

You begin shaking your head back and forth – almost uncontrollably. Finding new strength and standing up straight and tall, you ask a third time, addressing not your neighbor, but the entire room.

"WHAT IS THIS?," you shout, hearing your echo bounce off the giant wooden beams.

Without a single acknowledgement, you dart
toward the podium, then boomerang around the
sanctuary. As you run, yelling "HELLO?," you
notice your worst fear.

With a coffin opened halfway in the back corner,
you halt your hurry and stop a few feet away,
coming face–to–face with the body.

Quickly identifying the person lying inside, you
stop cold. You recognize them, even looking white
as snow.

Tucked neatly in the casket of the old church on a
sunny day lies the one who dreamed big but didn't
quite follow through; who had plans to live their
best life, but never took the first step; who
watched their childhood ideas drift further and
further as they grew up; who unsuccessfully
wanted to change the status quo and leave their
mark; who ignored their plans to build a career
that changed the world.

You recognize yourself.

Hitting your knees in despair, refusing to accept
you're an invisible bystander of your own funeral,
you begin calling to God for one more chance;
one more opportunity to try again, to do it right, to

follow the dreams you know you can achieve.

With your arms high and head low, you ask for one last, final chance, promising you'll make the most of each day to live those goals you ignored.

As you notice the pallbearers lifting the coffin — your coffin — and walking toward the door, you try one more time to be seen.

Running and jumping on the coffin, worried their exit would solidify your end, your weight slams the coffin to the floor and you feel your whole body thud atop the hard surface. Landing, your world grows dark and your eyes shut tight.

Feeling a sharp pain in the back of your head from the fall, you regain consciousness, hearing a bird chirp and a fan wisp.

Taking a few seconds to find your breathing, then gathering the strength to open your eyes, you find yourself lying on your bedroom floor, sheets and pillows astray. You stand up, realizing your funeral had been nothing but a dream – a silly old dream.

Standing up with a laugh of relief and looking out the window, you see a black hearse far off down the road, leaving your neighborhood.

A sense of spook crawling up your spine, you wonder if maybe — just maybe — it wasn't only a dream, but a wakeup call.

A wakeup call for life, liberty, and the pursuit of your dreams; those dreams to live that life, become that role model, and change the world.

A wake up call for another chance. A chance to be extraordinary; to become a life–giving leader in a world of monotony; and to be a happy, healthy, hearty forerunner trailblazing a happy, healthy, hearty legacy.

Opening the window and sticking your head toward the blue sky, you wink toward the heavens.

"Thank you," you whisper, knowing your talent, ability, and heart have much more to give the world.

As you read the chapters ahead — chapters of dreams fulfilled, brands built, and lives changed — imagine your days, starting today, as your second chance at life.

Envision yourself, starting now, saying yes instead of no — yes to every opportunity you once passed up.

Few get a second chance at life, and today is your chance.

Don't waste it.

Chapter 1:

Let There Be Light(bulbs)

"Hell, there ain't no rules around here! We're trying to accomplish something." – Thomas Edison

"Tommy, it's not that difficult. If you would just listen to me, you'd understand! Can't you think!? 3x4! Give me the answer!"

Seven-year-old Tommy, a horrified look on his face, couldn't think clearly.

The wrinkly-faced, red-cheeked Reverend Engle often put him on the spot, eyes seemingly ablaze. And in front of all his friends, the pressure burning his brain, Tommy could never quite scrounge up the answer.

"Umm, sir, it's, um…" Tommy did his best to clear his mind and calculate. He knew it wasn't a hard one, only…

"Tommy, now!" the reverend barked, eyes growing thinner and thinner like razor blades cutting into Tommy's thoughts.

"Sir, I can't think right now. You're making... making me nervous...," Tommy gulped, knowing the leather strap was on the reverend's desk menacingly waiting to red another bottom.

"You don't know, you say..." the revered questioned, slowly walking toward Tommy.

Clearing his throat and holding back tears, Tommy squeaked back, "n–no sir."

"You can't 'think' right now, you say..?" the reverend asked, taking another step.

Eyes wide as saucers and his heart pounding louder than a war drum, Tommy shook his head back and forth.

Standing over Tommy, twenty pairs of little eyes on the scene, Reverend Engle banged his fists on the desk.

"We have gone over and over this! You're exactly right about one thing – you truly are unable to think. You're addled, is what you are, an ill, confused little boy who can't think straight."

Tommy, nervously glancing at the leather strap he feared was nearing his future, didn't want to hear another word, jolting out of his chair and sprinting for the door before the man could stop him.

He was well-aware of his learning disability, and memorizing equations was pure torture. But he was trying as hard as he could and didn't deserve that strap – not today!

Home sounded like an oasis compared to the stuffy classroom, and he couldn't stay in there another second without bursting into tears in front of his friends.

Leaving his lunch pail behind and refusing to look back once, Tommy ran the long, dusty road home. It being early afternoon, he knew his mother – his favorite person alive – would be there preparing dinner or airing out the laundry.

Not seeing his mom in the yard, he erupted through the front door, calling to her. He panted with exhaustion and collapsed into his father's wooden rocking chair as she poked her head out of the kitchen.

"Tommy... why are you home, why are you so red... and what did you do?" she asked with a look mixing strict concern and unconditional love only a mother could manage.

Catching his breath, Tommy slowly replied. "Mother... is it true? Am I unable to think? Am I stupid?"

Shocked by the question, his mother walked over and crouched next to her son – her youngest of seven – her baby. "Honey, what on earth?"

"Instructor Engle said I'm useless, mother. In front of..." Tommy couldn't hold back the tears any longer, allowing them to freely flow. "In front of everyone."

Without missing a beat, his mother quietly answered him. "Honey, you listen to me very carefully," she said with a serious look and a squeeze of his hand, "you are not stupid, you are smart. In fact, some day, you're going to be a genius, you wait and see."

Fixing her son a snack and sending him into the yard to play, Tommy's mother decided she would visit Reverend Engle and get to the bottom of it herself. Tommy had always been a peculiar child, different than her other children, but she knew he had a uniqueness about him.

However, visiting the reverend the following day, she was told her son was **anything** but unique. In fact, she was informed he was just plain dumb – ill, to be exact.

Aghast at the brash barbarity of the man, she decided to take a firm stance, then and there pronouncing her son – her precious boy – would never step foot in that school, or any school, again.

Then onward, she warmly educated Tommy at their home, cunningly replacing scale and lesson memorization with hands–on learning for her dyslexic son. She broadened his philosophical horizons with books at a level far surpassing anyone his age, enlightening his philosophical compass.

As years passed, the unconventional learning continued, and Tommy continued to flourish. His appetite for knowledge grew, complete with days spent reading piles of books; his library was the forest, science lab the kitchen, and recess the farm fields.

Tommy's world became vivid once he realized — and truly believed — his mother was right. He was not stupid at all. He just did things a different way, his way.

Experimenting with ideas of his own and developing unrestricted styles of thinking by working solo, he discovered a desire to work with his hands – to create. And having ripened from a boy into a young man, his will–power grew right along with him.

Putting his unconventional wisdom to use, Tommy dabbled in creating new and often unforeseen doodads and gizmos. It was just his innate nature to build and conceive, as if he couldn't stop if he tried.

While it took some time to get his rhythm, his savvy flared at just twenty–two years old. Hoping to benefit as many people as possible, he focused on improving a world–wide device: the telegraph. Figuring he could enhance the way they printed, he designed the 'Universal Stock Printer' and won big.

A tremendous feat for a green inventor, Tommy acquired $40,000 overnight – worth over $1 million by today's standards.

Tommy's invention astounded the nation, and frankly – the fame astounded him, too. Deciding to not hang his hat but instead dive deeper, he continued to improve the world's "normal," each masterpiece more shocking than the last.

Light–bulb to movie camera, Tommy — or **Thomas Edison** — the former dyslexic "addled" child who "couldn't think," went on to become the most prolific thinker in American history.

"I remember never being able to get along at school (before my mother took over). I was always at the bottom of the class... my (own) father thought I was stupid," Edison shares about his youth.

Tommy's out–of–the–box life proves no matter how the world lives/leads/thinks, we don't have to follow along. Cloning others only makes us average.

Tommy could have stayed in that class as a young boy, fitting his square peg into a round hole, suffocated his unique gifts. However, little Tommy's first invention was as a seven–year–old boy: inventing the art of paving a unique trail, going against the grain of institutionalized learning.

We all have gifts and talents, shortcomings and downfalls. The problem with our world is focusing on becoming like 'everyone else,' taking the 'same path' as the majority. When in reality, those who excel choose the unbeaten road.

Outliers who think for themselves are the lucky few who develop a natural skill-set free of distraction or concern with what's "trendy."

Treks to success don't look identical one to the next, and in fact – the more unique the journey, the more unique the outcome. Yet often, we believe we must focus on what's expected, or else we're "cheating" life.

Instead, whatever comes natural, easy, and lights fire in our hearts is where we belong – where we should pitch out tents. That's our uniqueness. That's where we will succeed most, contrary to assuming we must live a specific way professionally, educationally, and personally to "fit in." Instead, the wise focus on becoming the "right fit."

Thomas, once deemed mentally-ill, was placed in

the wrong box. Once his learning was specialized to fit his gifts, his creativity was unleashed in ways no man could copy.

Like Thomas, our passions are unique. Our businesses are unique. Heck, **we** are unique. What works well for one may work horribly for another, and vice versa.

We play a leading role in mastering our own fate; the world has no right to provide us our script. We must question: are we living 'our' way and leading 'our' way, or attempting to become a cookie-cutter of the norm?

"There's a way to do it better – find it," Edison explained. Knowing this, how can we — each uniquely invented by OUR Creator — find our 'better' way?

Whether you, reading this, are an elephant or donkey in the political realm, both parties have wisdom on this mindset.

President Donald Trump coined the phrase "you cannot compete at the highest level of your industry unless you're deeply passionate about what you do." The lucky, like Trump explained, are those whose passions aligns perfectly with their career.

Hillary Clinton, during her 1969 commencement speech as a twenty–two year old graduate, shared how "we are, all of us, exploring a world that none of us even understands (yet) attempting to create within that uncertainty." She understood the importance of reaching for the stars with all question marks aside.

Yet unfortunately, the majority of the world doesn't live the reality Trump and Clinton explained.

Recently, there was an image shared on Facebook over one million times proving this concept. The picture showed a man casually walking into a room and seeing a printer on fire. He immediately left as if he'd seen nothing. Underneath, it said "this is me when there's a problem at work, but I don't get paid enough to care."

That photo sums it all up: those with passion for their work, whether CEO or part–time receptionist, will get their hands dirty no matter the stickiness. Those without passion will not.

When we look at our lifespan at 30,000 feet – like an airplane flying overhead – we realize it's quite short. We have about 29,000 days on planet Earth, so how do we plan to use them? By fixing the situation... or just leaving the room?

While the world wants to tell us how to live our life — we need to remember, it's just that, OURS. Success follows passion, and a passionate life cannot exist when boundaries are set.

There's always a purpose and way to make our lives a little better, because — frankly — we'll never get them back. Today is the day to begin, for the sake of our tomorrows.

Dunder Mifflin's Andy Bernard (i.e. *The Office*) wrapped a worldwide fear with a big, red bow: **"I wish there was some way to know we're in the good old days before we leave them."**

Although Andy's words were dripping with sarcasm in the sitcom scene, they ring genuine: **we are living in our good old days.**

This day will one day be our past, and the times we remember, really remember, are those embracing purpose, passion, and the pursuit of happiness for ourselves, and more importantly – others.

The CEO's and leaders we will discover and study in the 'life manual' you're currently holding were/ are jolly, humble, and once — ordinary. And besides exclusively having existential evidence on paper, they leave a mark somewhere eternal: hearts.

Your tomorrow starts today – so pull down your lap bar on this lifelong roller coaster and begin stirring your spirit with zest. Your life is your life, your company is your company; your ride.

Now have a blast, live it up, work harder than before, and make us proud. And like the famous Thomas Edison spoke, **"If we did all the things we were capable of, we would literally astound ourselves."**

How can you astound yourself today?

Chapter 2:

Double Tall Skinny Decaf Latte

"I can't imagine a day without coffee. I can't imagine!" – Howard Schultz, Starbucks Owner

As the concrete jungle bustled with cars, tourists, and vendors outside the window, Howard, safe inside the diner, looked down at his toes.

The Brooklyn-bred middle schooler thought again about his father, whom was let go from his job due to a work injury and hadn't been the same for a while.

Juggling desperation and reality, the twelve-year-old envisioned turning things around for his family... to show them how much he cared, for his father, especially.

"Order up, boy! Anotha' coffee, black," Howard heard – snapping him out of his thoughts.

In one swift motion, almost robotically, Howard grabbed a white mug, poured the hot liquid, stuck it on a saucer and slid the cup down the counter toward the customer.

He'd recently landed a job serving locals at a small cafe. It wasn't a *bad* gig. He wasn't out shooting hoops or running touchdowns with his buddies, but he *was* making money. Plus, he knew if he *was* out playing, he'd win (being the best baller on the block and all).

Still holding the clear coffee pot, Howard looked down at the black goo. He'd never tried the stuff and didn't quite understand the hype. His parents drank it. Most customers ordered a hot cup upon entrance. But everything, look to smell, just didn't sit right with the pre-teen.

Setting the pot down on the burner, Howard shrugged and ventured into his thoughts yet again. He'd be successful beyond just pouring coffee someday, right?

"Two more 'joes over here, sonny," Howard heard, who – in a matter of seconds – had full cups slid down the opposite side of the counter.

Throughout Howard's middle and high school years, whether in the cafe or out and about, he continued dreaming about his "someday."

As the years flew by, his dreams for success didn't wither. And with a glimmer of hope landing a 9–5 selling European appliances after college, he hoped to be well on his way toward achieving them.

His days were pretty typical. The company specialized in drip–coffee makers, and his customers consisted of retail stores around the country. He made habitual calls, took sales trips here and there, and earned a decently generous paycheck. Far from groundbreaking, it didn't *exactly* 'get his blood moving,' so to speak.

Until one day, that is, when everything changed. Sitting at his desk making habitual calls and scanning his monthly reports, something caught his eye; something peculiar.

One of his customers, a startup coffee operation out of Seattle, had an unusual habit of ordering **obscene amounts** of coffee makers, surpassing even Macy's. Quarter after quarter, the company ordered more and more, and it didn't add up.

Making his quarterly call to that particular shop,
Starbucks Coffee, Tea & Spice, they answered his
probing questions kindly: "Well son, come to
Seattle and see the fun for yourself!"

Feeling young and adventurous, he shrugged his
shoulders. Chuckling a little, his response
solidified the invitation, "you know, I've never
been to Seattle," a smile forming on the corners
of his mouth.

Stepping into the Seattle shop a few weeks later,
a deep aroma of mocha encompassing the air, he
didn't quite know what he was doing there. Upon
his first few steps, however, that changed.

Feeling an odd sense of familiarity, a déjà vu of
sorts, he felt – strange as it sounded – like he was
home.

Rain lightly pitter–pattering the windows, burlap
coffee bags stacked along the walls, and free
samples of bean flavors placed neatly on the
counter, Howard saw his European coffee makers
greeting customers front and center.

Grabbing for a sample of the nearest cup,
Howard's eyes grew wide. Even after years of
long nights in college and the professional world,

Howard felt no different about coffee than the disgust he'd felt as a Brooklyn pre-teen, until this particular drizzly Seattle afternoon. Finishing the cup and grabbing another, Howard was shocked at the smooth, satisfying taste – nothing like the bitter gunk he'd choked down in the past.

Feeling a warmness inside the store, located right outside the energetic Pike Place Market, Howard could feel something deep down whispering to him: "Howard, this is where you belong."

Upon meeting the founders face-to-face, Howard learned about its genesis. The trio, consisting of two former teachers and a writer whom had met in college, started the company ten years prior and opened six stores throughout Seattle selling coffee beans acquired from world-wide farmers.

Choosing 'Starbucks' as the title, referring to the twin-tailed mermaid in Herman Melville's novel *Moby Dick*, the founders developed their logo and brand based on her character.

Within minutes, Howard felt like a hooked fish.

"This is something I've been looking for my whole professional life," Howard confessed.

Refusing a "no," Howard offered – quite convincingly – his services as Director of Marketing.

Spellbound by his confident demeanor and communicative prowess, the founders agreed to the request, and Howard was officially on board.

Knowing this could be his 'espresso shot' at success, he treated the company as if it were his own, recognizing how although it was great, there was room for sharpening.

After a few months in Seattle, Howard booked a flight to Milan to muse over the lively coffee culture he'd heard about via the caffeine–world grapevine. Arriving – he was astonished, finding it grander than anticipated.

Brimming with cafes, Milan reflected not only the romance of coffee, but a sense of community surrounding those hot cups. Coffee didn't just enhance the culture, coffee *was* the culture.

Most surprising was how coffee shops in Milan weren't just mini–markets, but hubs for social meetings and leisure. In the United States, the socializing role was mostly held by various fast–food restaurants, and Howard knew this new concept could change everything for Starbucks.

He recognized something special; **humans, whether Italian or Seattleites, were desperate for community and love. If Starbucks could deliver that, the opportunities for clientele was endless.**

After a week of research in Italy, thirty–year–old Howard was convinced – with unbridled enthusiasm – Starbucks should shift from selling whole beans to selling individual drinks. Although the idea of 'coffee by the cup' was foreign in Seattle, Howard knew with the right atmosphere, baristas, and marketing – it could, and **would**, be a hit.

Quickly gathering the owners to illustrate his travels and share the recipes he'd learned for lattes and cappuccinos, he explained his idea. "Guys, this is the new direction. This is what we need to develop — coffee bars!"

Anticipating equal enthusiasm, Howard was sorely disappointed, as their reactions were far from thrilled.

"Oh no, that's not for us, Howard. We're in the bean business, plain and simple. Real coffee is made at home!"

Discouraged yet adamant, Howard's new dream was so entrenched in his heart, he wouldn't let it go. He brought it up day after day, knowing it was the secret ingredient to their business plan.

The trio finally relented, allowing for a coffee bar at just one of their six locations simply to appease him. Lo and behold, his idea worked.

The location was an instant success with hundreds of customers a day, launching a new category of joy in Seattle — the dawning of the true coffeehouse.

Pointing to the success of that location, the delighted Howard was shocked when the trio still shook their heads, explaining they didn't want to 'go big,' afraid to lose the charm of their small community and original plan focused on the beans.

Crushed as ground coffee, Howard felt no path but to kindly resign, accepting how the coffee culture of Seattle was in his hands alone.

Contrary to lacking monetary resources, Howard did not lack enthusiasm. "Only those taking unexplored roads build a long-lasting company," he told himself, marching into a local bank.

Borrowing $400,000, Howard opened his own Italian–breathed coffee bar, 'Il Giornale,' (named after an Italian newspaper) finding popularity quickly with 300 visitors on just the first day, all the while granting himself, at thirty–three years old, the leadership experience of running his own company.

As if by divine intervention, the Starbucks trio put their brand and stores on the market one year later, and Howard knew it was destiny. Loaning another $4 million from creditors and investors (including Bill Gates), Howard became the sole owner of Starbucks.

Rebounding to Italy for another week, Howard noticed how the Italian baristas put on — quite literally — a theatrical presentation. They poured espresso with one hand, whipped cream with the other, and chatted with the customers — all at the same time.

Returning to Seattle two weeks later with Italian menus, videos of the baristas, and new ideas, Howard turned the Starbucks brand into an Italian oasis.

Successfully teaching his baristas to have finesse yet personality, Seattle became known as the country's coffee haven where caffeine brewed the spirit of community and life.

Howard turned coffee into an elegant product, an art. While any would deem it difficult – in the early 1980's – to lure people to a place with no smoking and nothing but the smell of freshly brewed coffee, Howard's avant–garde ideas proved to be progressive enough to acquire loyal customers.

Howard created a democratic coffee house where the customer was king; where the type of drink (coffee, latte, cappuccino, espresso, mocha, macchiato), size (tall, venti, grande), temperate (hot, iced), and milk (creamer, 2%, nonfat, non–dairy) gave individual customers their 'Starbucks ID,' so to speak.

Howard's freshly–hired marketing team was constantly spreading how drinking the right coffee is romantic, using slogans like: 'it's not just coffee, it's Starbucks,' 'perfect with something (or someone) sweet,' or 'the alarm clock you drink in a cup.'

Following his onslaught in Seattle, Howard studied the McDonald's model of business and began opening stores in other markets, starting in New England and working West.

Soon, with an amplifying company and more employees than he could count, Howard instated medical insurance, company share, and even college payment for his employees — strategically named 'partners.'

Today, Howard is worth $2.2 billion dollars, employs 200,000+ partners at 25,000+ stores worldwide, and owns a brand generating north of $20 billion annually.

Howard Schultz generated charm out of the glorified 'liquid goo' he served at the New York City cafe at twelve years old. His sense of branding and storytelling literally changed the perception of date–night, self–care, and 'treating oneself,' standing out as the superior 'enchantment' chain in all the world.

His success resulted from the **brand clarity** he provided to the market. The products (coffee and light fair) and clientele (anyone needing 'love in a mug') were both clear. Everyone knew who exactly belonged as a customer and why.

Most fail to succeed like Schultz, finding

themselves unable to achieve leverage in the marketplace, due to one main problem: an **unclear brand.** An unclear brand means no one knows who belongs there or what the main product/service is, and therefore: **no one cares.**

Many owners do too much too quickly, leading to demise. With too much too soon, no one understands exactly what the business is or whom it serves. With a jumbled message, the 'perfect customer' will not know they belong, and hence, they won't come.

Often, business owners who lose money at the start tend to tack more services onto the existing business thinking it will make the company more marketable. In reality, they should cut the unprofitable services instead of simply adding new ones.

Services offered by a company are a lot like a wardrobe. Before buying a new coat (adding a service), it's important to look in the current closet and consider ridding of one or two coats (services that aren't wildly successful).

A clear brand is necessary for a "boom" in the marketplace. With too many messages, no one hears a thing. Overcomplicating the brand is the achilles heel for thousands of businesses who fail to find their niche.

No amount of marketing can fix a broken brand, yet branding is often overlooked from the get–go because, bluntly, people don't even know what a brand is.

A brand distinguishes an organization from its rivals in the eyes of the customer. Everyone has a brand whether they know it or not. Smart companies craft it themselves, but most allow it to organically occur based on word–of–mouth or reputation.

Providing clarity reshapes convoluted brand messages. The clearer the branding, the clearer the customer base. Either a business has a clear brand that spreads, or they become irrelevant.

Branding includes:

1. Understanding your mission: Through developing an adjective list describing the personality of your company, service, staff, and mission, you will develop your main focus. Using words like 'friendly, responsive, service–minded, classy, etc' can make a clear path stating your strong points. What do you want to be known for?

2. Distinguishing your perfect customer: If no one pays for the services your company provides, or they don't understand your niche, back up. Discover your perfect customer and find a need they deem unmet. On a practical level, who is it you want to do business with?

3. Flexibility to adapt: The chief advantage in business is having an ability to attack profit pools faster than competition. If there's opportunity and value in a new market, dive in. This begins with understanding the evolving needs of your perfect customer.

4. Simplification: Instead of starting/running a business with many services, which can get confusing, start with a main focus. The secret sauce of business is not to over-complicate things too early and to remove things when necessary.

Now, Build Your Brand!

Howard himself put it best: "I am convinced most people can achieve their dreams – and beyond – if they have the determination to keep trying."

With the right branding, you can achieve those

professional dreams.

Only question is, are you determined to keep trying?

Paige Weslaski

Chapter 3:

Float Like A Butterfly

"I'm not the greatest; I'm the double greatest.
Not only do I knock 'em out, I pick the round."
– Muhammad Ali

Pulling up his signature white shorts and breathing deeply in the locker room, Cassius Clay was (almost) ready. It was 1964, and he'd read in the morning papers he was about to participate in the "fight of his life."

He wasn't the best fighter in the world, just a boxer with a mean grit and coach who believed in him. But he *sure knew* he was strong, and he *sure knew* he could tear down anyone who undermined that.

Hearing the announcer rile up the crowd, he stood up from the bench slowly and beat his chest a few times. The sportswriters could say all they wanted about the fight, like how he'd get pummeled by the infamous Sonny Liston. Sure, his competitor Sonny was the 'heavyweight champion of the world.' But that's because he didn't yet know Clay.

Clay was told 43 out of the 46 sportswriters were betting against him, and that the majority of the crowd had their money against him, too. In fact, bets were less about Sonny winning and more about how many rounds it would take to knockout Clay.

Clay hit his arms a few times as he jumped up and down preparing for the fight. "I am the best. I am the best. I am the best," he thought over and over and over, almost fanatically.

He made his way toward the door, walked toward the main arena, and felt the warmth of the spotlight find him in the doorway.

"May we present to you…Cassius Clay!!!!" the announcer boomed.

Meanwhile, half the crowd went wild with chants, "Kill Em Clay! Kill Em Clay!" with the others yelling "Son–ny! Son–ny!"

Taking in the moment for just a second, Clay knew he had it in him, it was his destiny. They called Sonny "the best," but Clay would be better.

Walking up toward the ring, each step stronger than the last, he found his coach, confidante, and best friend Dundee awaiting him.

"THIS is what you have been training for. He doesn't even KNOW how strong you are. He doesn't even KNOW how fast you are. He doesn't even KNOW who you ARE!" Coach Dundee whirred while squeezing Clay's shoulders.

Both men riled and ready as could be and the announcer beckoning the fighters to their positions, Coach Dundee stopped Clay before he jumped into the ring.

"Hey, Clay!" he shouted as he grabbed Clay's shoulder. Pulling a small notepad and pen out of his pocket, he wrote a number down and stuck it into Clay's glove.

"That's how many rounds it'll take you to beat him. You will win, Clay."

Following one more nod, Clay jumped into the

ring, going on to beat Sonny Liston in seven rounds. It was deemed one of the biggest upsets in boxing history.

And just one week later, Cassius Clay was renamed Muhammad Ali, the greatest boxer who ever lived.

Ali was and is the greatest, but he did not accomplish his goals alone. His biggest supporter, Coach Dundee, was just as certain about Ali's ability, if not more-so, slipping a small piece of paper into Ali's glove before every boxing match. Dundee was so confident in Ali's ability, he wasn't guessing whether or not Ali would win. He guessed *when* he would win.

Ali's trainer had full confidence in him, no doubt playing a tremendous effect in his success. Coach Dundee was sure, without-a-doubt, Ali would succeed, aiding Ali's "champion" mentality.

And not unlike Ali, every great leader is surrounded by great supporters.

Even when the outcome may be uncertain, knowing a team has your back works wonders in the cut-throat world of business. Victory comes with a capable, confident team.

In a business setting, owners set the tone of the direction and mission, and teams follow suit. However, time and time again, a team – no matter how strong – can be underutilized and under-appreciated by an unhappy, incapable, or unmotivated leader.

There's no doubt Ali would've been wildly successful even without Coach Dundee, but Dundee only strengthened the matches through his assurance, vigorous training programs, and paper slips. A person of inner strength, like Ali, attracts the right "squad."

Before correctly building a team of Coach Dundee clones to work alongside you (which we'll get to later in the chapter), a leader must be strong on his/her own – like Ali. And this, without question, begins with how one's life is lived.

Strong leaders are generally passionate leaders. The key to developing a mentality of a leader is through searching for passion the correct way.

To break it down. There's three ways to pursue your passion as a leader: **living a pleasant life, an engaged life, or a meaningful life.**

The **'pleasant life'** is hedonistic, wherein you engage – frequently and consistently – in what gives you instant pleasure. Eating a favorite food, watching a favorite TV show, playing video games... you name it, you do it.

The **'engaged life'** is a step up from the 'pleasant life,' where you cultivate your strengths (whether involving love, work, etc) to enhance your own, personal life.

The **'meaningful life'** represents using your talents to better not just your life, but the world. You consistently (and proactively) work toward helping a greater cause, be it a political party, faith, family, cause, or community.

Psychologist Martin Seligman of the University of Pennsylvania discovered the happiest two groups out of the three above. Can you take a guess?

The first group, those living 'pleasant lives,' were much less happy compared to the other two groups, with the 'meaningful lifers' being the happiest.

His study was clear: **those who pursue what they love and witness that positive impact on the world are able to better themselves and the**

world around them – leading to long–term passion/happiness. He realized passionate people are intentional about their work and their time, marking their calendars with habitual plans that promote their strengths and their positive mark on others.

As a business leader, it's crucial to not only manage a business you find passion in, but to also create a culture where the staff knows they're bettering the world one way or another. **Successful leaders create successful employees which create successful clients which create successful sales.**

The right mentality as a leader is important, but being surrounded by a strong team is equally critical. Every team member must understand, carry out, and truly believe the mission in order for the business to run like a well–oiled machine.

Walt Disney, of whom we'll study in–depth in a later chapter, instituted steep hiring requirements for his parks, still followed to this day. This process especially pertains to their most coveted position: the Disneyland Princess.

One Disneyland Princess, Belle from *Beauty and the Beast* to be exact, described how extensive and cut-throat the selection process was:

"We started with five-hundred girls, lined up in rows of about ten. The casting directors went up and down the rows, immediately cutting most girls based on whether or not they looked like 'Belle.' They measured us twice to make sure we fit the height (5'3"– 5'7"), took lots of pictures, and taught us a dance to gauge your gracefulness. By the end, there were seven girls still there. Somehow, they eventually picked me as their girl."

Mr. Disney knew he couldn't single-handedly create a magical destination empire; he would need dynamite employees by his side – the prettiest of princesses, no less.

The hiring process for Disney, and all companies in general, is a big deal. Princess, painter, paralegal… no matter the industry, hiring is the most important job of any leader.

Forbes pegs the cost of a bad hire anywhere between $25,000–$50,000 when the cost of finding, interviewing, engaging, and training is factored in, not counting the computer, desk, and more.

Smart leaders hire smarter than themselves. "I

hire people brighter than me, and then I get out of their way," the former president of Ford Motors once said. Hiring the right team can make or break a business. In a sense, a company is only as strong as its weakest employee.

Step one before hiring a productive, powerhouse staff is knowing exactly what you need, a trait online conglomerate Google has mastered.

Google receives about two million job applications every year, only hiring four–thousand of those people; hence making it harder to work for Google than to get into Harvard or Yale.

And they know exactly how to funnel those two million applications into hires: Googleyness. Yes, it's a real thing. **Here's what Googley people have:**

"...attributes like **enjoying fun** (who doesn't), a certain dose of **intellectual humility** (it's hard to learn if you can't admit you might be wrong), a strong measure of **conscientiousness** (we want owners, not employees), comfort with **ambiguity** (we don't know how our business will evolve), and **evidence they've taken some courageous or interesting paths in life.**"

The head of HR explained how "Google **doesn't care if you were the President of your chess club in high school** or if you made a beeline to becoming a sales executive. The more important thing is to know when you should step in and display leadership (or) step back when you shouldn't."

Google understands its culture and mission, hiring accordingly. They aren't afraid to stump candidates with interview questions, having asked the following in the past:

– **Estimate the number of tennis balls that can fit into a plane.**
– **Tell me a joke.**
– **If you could be remembered for one sentence, what would it be?**
– **How would you solve homelessness in downtown San Francisco?**
– **If you could choose one song that would play when you walked into a room for the rest of your life, what would it be?**
– **Tell me something about you that's not on your resume.**
– **What scares you?**
– **What would you do if you didn't have to work?**
– **Name a prank you would pull on 'x' manager if you were hired.**

– Do you prefer earning or learning?
– How many cars travel across a bridge each day?

Google's been known for asking brain–teaser questions primarily to see if candidates can think on their feet and tackle problems on the spot. Wit to wisdom, Google wants it all.

When choosing who to hire, listen to your gut and your brain. And step two, tougher than even the first, is keeping them around.

Young talent will not make a life–long career at a company they don't feel personally attached to, and a genuine sense of care from the managerial staff benefits retention. Once your solid team is secured, stride toward keeping them.

One California startup awards funny trophies to standouts. This includes the **"Guy in a Suit"** trophy to the top sales member, and a **"Makin' the Bacon"** medal to the 'Employee of the Month.' They love passing the awards around the office, creating an inclusive culture within the company tribe.

Another business leader was deeply motivated to keep his millennial staff for good, hosting an **in–**

house happy hour every Friday. The office un-officially "closes" early, yet his employees stay on the clock for the extra time, eating healthy snacks and sipping on local craft beers.

"It's a great way to end the week on a positive note and doesn't cost much compared to the benefits it provides," the CEO explained.

Another company provides a similar outlet. "It's called our **Eatin' Meetin'**. Besides sharing a good cabernet, it's an hour set aside on Fridays where the whole team gets together to talk about accomplishments (or failures) for the week. It's a simple perk our team loves."

These companies get it: they lead not only a business, but a family. An all-staff motivational **book club**, holiday **potlucks**, a friendly **app competition** such as "Heads Up," **volleyball** or **bowling**, or simply a group **coffee run** around the block can boost even the mousiest of employees to feel part of the exclusive business tribe.

One CEO named Jason, a former fitness coach, even decided to incorporate **workouts** into his team-bonding activities. "I haven't encountered an activity that will bring a team or group closer together than a good, old-fashioned group workout!"

Blair Thomas of eMerchantBroker chose **volunteering** as his avenue: "Spending a few hours at a soup kitchen, gathering toys for needy children, or organizing a community cleanup brings teams together. Employees get the warm feeling of helping others, and it gives your team a chance to get to know each other and work together outside the office."

Fun – in any capacity – generates closeness. Closeness generates pride. Pride generates retention. Retention generates an enviable company culture.

BUILD BONDS

With multiple company divisions, closeness amongst an entire organization can grow difficult; as can happen with organizations of 50+ people. A fun, unique way to establish professional intimacy amongst these divisions is to grant each division a "team name."

One CEO gave each division a different superhero name, providing them Friday office–wear swag with a corresponding logo and color scheme. Team Batman (sales), Team Flash (techs), and the

Punishers (HR) enjoy donning their hero–attire.

Each "team" has their own inner–division bonding activities, and for the company–wide events they often play games against the other squads.

PROMOTE OWNERSHIP

A voice actively listened to produces ownership and team pride.

One Midwest media company currently has an employee of Puerto Rican descent with family on the island, so when Hurricane Maria pummeled the area and he didn't hear from them for two weeks, he knew he needed to help.

Asking his boss for a week off to serve in Puerto Rico, the boss didn't say 'yes.' Instead, he said 'count me in,' joining his employee as well as a handful of other co–workers for a week of dispensing supplies and hope to the people of Puerto Rico. All participating employees were given extra vacation time through the trip.

NOURISH, PRUNE, AND PAY

Jack Welch, former CEO of GE known for raising company value by 4,000%, explained the importance of 'pruning.'

"My main job was developing talent. I was a gardener providing water and other nourishment to our top 750 people. Of course, I had to pull out some weeds, too," said Welch.

Similarly, you are the gardener of your organization. Planting the right seeds, watering regularly, and clearing out the weeds creates a healthy garden.

But no "business garden" is sustained without an open checkbook, too. Businessman Robert Bosch was known for his famous quote: **"I don't pay good wages because I have a lot of money; I have a lot of money because I pay good wages."** Providing regular raises, bonuses, and generous incentives should not be overlooked.

And, last but not least, a wise leader provides adequate vacation days.

The average U.S. worker receives ten paid vacation days a year, while the average in Europe is twenty. Some E.U. countries have even upped the requirement to twenty–five and thirty days.

Many companies nowadays even provide unlimited

vacation! Don't be afraid to let them fly for a few extra days so they continue to return instead of ditch the coop for good.

THE COCKTAIL FOR SUCCESS

Want to be successful? Hire well. Want less headaches? Keep them happy. Want them for good? Pay well. Want them refreshed? Give them a life.

Provide your employees a sense of pride, a feeling of staff unity, room for personal growth, and the right paycheck, and you'll find yourself smooth sailing to success.

With a durable team beside you, you may go from a Cassius Clay to Muhammad Ali overnight.

Chapter Four:

Communes & Air Balloons

"My favorite mode of transport is air ballooning. It's so graceful to be blown by the wind, to go where the wind takes you." — Richard Branson, stepping aboard an air balloon

Peeping out of the square window, Richie was mesmerized by the birds.

Watching as the pack soared through the clouds, he noticed two robins suddenly fly off by themselves, taking turns playing tag before landing on a branch near the window.

"Someday, I'm gonna fly, too," he mused, as the robins left the branch and drifted into the distance.

"Richard Charles! Are you paying no attention at all?" his teacher scolded in front of the class, standing directly at Richie's small, wooden desk.

Nodding his head 'yes,' then shaking it 'no,' thirteen-year-old Richie found himself transported back to prep-school reality.

As the teacher beelined back to the chalkboard to continue his lesson on God-knows-what, Richie, who struggled with dyslexia, drifted yet again, side-glancing at the adjacent student taking vigorous notes on the lifeless grammar lesson.

Richie found his daydreams disrupted on too regular a basis. He'd mastered the art of daydreaming at his prestigious academy in Surrey, feeling less than interested in anything school related. His teachers, unfortunately, didn't approve of this newfound talent.

There *was* one thing Richie learned clear as day while attending his classes, however — he wanted out. He wouldn't become successful listening to lectures about statistics and ancient Greek literature. That, he knew, was a given.

As the years streamed by and his passion for school didn't make much improvement, he decided, officially, he'd had about enough. Passionless for academia yet boundlessly passionate about life, he reasoned his schedule fancied a little remodeling.

Packing his bags with London-town on his mind, sixteen-year-old Richie had no more than a few bucks in his pocket. But deep down, he felt selfishly rich with ideas. And that, he deemed, was quite enough for him.

Walking gallantly toward the front door of his boarding school to make his grand exit, he was **finally free.**

A fire lit under his butt to prove he'd made the right decision, he promptly got to work creating "Student," a youth-culture magazine. Run and written entirely by other students his age, the first edition was released just months after his dropping out of boarding school, selling 50,000 copies and generating $8,000 in advertising.

Living within a commune downtown, surrounded by the British music and party scene, Richie soaked up all London had to offer. Late nights, parties, and networking replaced homework, and Richie thrived in all things fast and reckless.

Naturally grasping the ins and outs of British Rock N' Roll, he, over time, was coined a 'go-to' for 'who was who' in the underground music scene.

The trendy Richie was becoming quite the key-player with his prominent magazine, and by twenty-three, he knew it was time to conquer a new battle. And with his amplifying bank account and newfound music knowledge, he shot a pricey dart into the unknown by opening a recording studio.

Selecting "Virgin Records" as its title, he found the adjective fitting, being a beginner to the professional industry. But in actuality, he found his green resume an advantage compared to washed up, tenured executives. Fresh eyes meant fresh talent.

And after his first client, Mike Oldfield, struck gold with a top-chart song, Richie was immediately stamped 'legitimate' in the music world.

The young, intuitive Richie began signing groups left and right, including the Sex Pistols, Genesis, Janet Jackson, and the Rolling Stones. Before he knew it, Richie's label grew into one of the top records in the entire world, all due to following his gut and quitting prep school as a teenage dreamer.

Not only was Richie creating superstars, he was starting to become one, too. Often stopped on the street for an autograph or words of encouragement, Richie's world was flipped upside-down, achieving unforeseen fame making it difficult to walk down Piccadilly without a stream of women at his tail.

Living every young man's dream, he knew he'd 'made it,' but not far enough, recalling those birds outside his window in prep school.

With a prayer, friend, and an incredible wit to fly, Richie – then a universal household name at age thirty-six – boarded an air balloon with the intent of setting a Guinness World Record.

Planning to cross the Atlantic Ocean from Maine to Ireland, his friends and family called him nuts. Shrugging his shoulders in response, he figured it wasn't his first bold move and wouldn't be his last, successfully completing the mission in a thick Irish fog.

Climbing out of the basket with a grin, Richie, once coined "unteachable" in prep-school, was now the worldwide kingpin of success.

As thirty-six turned to forty, fifty, and sixty,

Richie, better known as **Richard Branson**, went on to create a billion dollar airline, mobile phone company, train/cruise/hotel line, and space-tourism platform for Virgin.

Richard recognized his strengths early; he thrived detecting **possibility in the impossible**. He followed his entrepreneurial heart, even as a rebuked daydreamer in prep school.

Although once a 'virgin' in the eyes of the professional world, he quickly showed those professionals who was boss. Playing on his weaknesses by titling his company a name the world deemed as 'amateur,' he flipped the mindset that **novices – when motivated enough – could darn-well excel in any industry they chose.**

Yet unlike Richie, **people often lose sight of the "what if" because they're consumed with the "what is."** In his case, if he would have focused solely on the "what is," he would have lost out on a lifetime of success. Do you, unlike Richie, focus only on the "what is?"

Try something with me: examine your life as if you're looking through another person's eyes, and be honest. Are you "following the rules" of society a little too closely? Grinding through your days with a different passion in your heart? Living a life you find unfulfilling? Dreading getting out of bed each dawn?

The most successful people have one thing in common: they are incredibly passionate about what they do. **One cannot compete at the highest level of business, or life for that matter, without being deeply passionate about that which they're running toward.**

Those who 'win' in life, who receive the gold medal or build the business empire or simply smile on their drive to work, aren't always those you'd immediately expect. Richie is example #1, having 'willed his way' toward his wins.

There's an acclaimed sports quote used by world-renowned competitors agreeing with this concept: **"the mind is the athlete."** Not the body, not ingrained talent — the mind.

There's no doubt this quote works just as well – if not better – in the business world, seeing as Wall Street doesn't care how tall we are, how many miles we can run, or how high we can('t) jump. **We decide how far to go; it's determined by our will and wit alone.**

Often, we assume heroes within both the business and athletic worlds are just "born with it," as if they've received a hidden "it-factor" to "make it" in life. According to the winners themselves, that's false.

Muhammad Ali says it all: **"I hated every minute of training, but I said, 'Don't quit. Suffer now and live the rest of your life as a champion.'"**

And Babe Ruth agrees: **"It's hard to beat the person who never gives up."**

It's no question some are born with special talents or silver spoons or trust funds, and sure — those traits can obviously be a stepping stool into success. But in professional success, just like in athletics, hard work beats talent when talent fails to work hard.

Mark Cuban, the 'working-class hustler' turned 'billionaire-mogul' featured on CNBC's *Shark Tank*, similarly concurs: **"No one had high hopes for me. I came from a working class family... but I was a hustler. Success is not about money or connections. It's the willingness to outwork and outlearn everyone when it comes to your business. If it fails, you learn from what happened and do a better job next time."**

Cuban is a prime example of trying, learning, and moving on. His first business venture was a bar he bought in college, having raised $15,000 through loans from his buddies. The bar, named 'Motley's,' was an immediate hit. That is, until it came crashing down via a wet t–shirt contest gone wrong. However, just because his 'Plan A' didn't work, he knew there were twenty–five more metaphorical letters to try.

Our world is full of willing people: some willing to do the work, the rest willing to let them. Cuban, like Richie, was willing to do it ALL so he'd never have to work for somebody. He bounced back from the bar catastrophe by creating a software company and sold it a few years later for a whopping six million dollars. Afterwards, he decided to retire early to fly around the world on a quest to see as many countries as he could.

But, 'an entrepreneur once, an entrepreneur for life,' they say, and the unorthodox "Mark–the–Shark" couldn't stay out of the game long; eventually diving back in and accumulating billions, becoming a reality–star in the process.

The thrills of an entrepreneurial–lifestyle fly at a speed few can outrun. The exhilaration of changing the world and climbing to the top is enough to get anyone's blood moving, and the chase for professional success is the most addicting drug of choice.

Lucrative leaders, like Richard or Cuban or others, are often known for exhibiting over-the-top enthusiasm and even obsessive traits at times. Uber-successful people are not average, and it takes a specific type of person to succeed at the art of visioning, creating, and leading a successful business.

Constructing a thriving brand has been compared to jumping off a cliff and building an airplane on the way down. Many people are afraid to jump; and many who *do* jump don't know how to build a plane. The real warriors – the ones who become their own pilot and fly their company into the sunset, are not cheap to come by.

Perhaps the brave Amelia Earhart shared it best. Etched on the side of the plane she flew across the Atlantic, it said this: "Always think with your stick forward."

Her reasoning was if she slowed down, she would crash. But if she kept the plane's stick forward, thinking positively, trusting should could do it —

she would (and did).

Starting a business is a lot like flying a plane (or hot air balloon, like Richie!) for 15 hours over an ocean; it's scary, it's not necessary (as there's always a cozy spot in corporate America), and it takes guts. But thinking with our stick forward removes procrastination and hesitation, getting us moving.

However, before taking the initial jump, building a plane, and flying over the ocean, **we need to know the type of leaders we are.** Knowing our strengths and weaknesses paves for better planning, and furthermore, a more precise "passenger list" – or "staff."

Self–awareness is useful in developing the DNA of a company culture, and step one is to develop your personal **'Leadership IQ.'** Through the following test, you'll pinpoint your own, personal Leadership IQ rating. Rate yourself 1–10 for the following six questions:

1. How do you feel about risk?
(1: you stay far away from risk; 10: 'Superman' is your middle name)
2. How do you feel about change?
(1: you keep the status quo; 10: you're a gecko)

3. How many new ideas pop into your brain compared to others?
(1: not many; 10: too many to be normal)
4. How whimsical are you?
(1: you're too steady for that nonsense; 10: you're far from being a 'bore')
5. How's your relationship to ambiguity?
(1: you need a game-plan; 10: you crave 'unknown territory')
6. How do you feel regarding new opportunity?
(1: you'd rather stay home; 10: "YOLO")

Add your answers and divide them by 6 for your answer. Next, we'll dissect your mentality:

1–5: You're a concrete thinker. You think literally, and you're focused on the physical world of what you KNOW to be true and KNOW will work based on your past. You're focused on facts in the here and now, physical objects, and literal definitions.

6–10: You're an abstract thinker. You have the ability to think about objects, principles, and ideas not physically present, such as success for a future company others could be unsure about.

Now, let's get even more specialized with your number:

1–2 (the "grinders"): Grinders like to be given a task and just grind out the work. They don't like thinking too much about the "what ifs," and they make great employees.

3–4 (the "minders"): Minders can manage a small group of people and are very well organized. Minders can "manage the store," so to speak.

5–6 (the "keepers"): Keepers are great with people, somewhat focused on detail, and can generally think both logically and abstractly.

7–8 (the "finders"): Finders are abstract thinkers who aren't concerned with much detail. They like having concrete thinkers around them, they can spot opportunity, and they like new challenges.

9–10 (the "conceivers"): Conceivers are bright, persuasive entrepreneurs. Conceivers rarely work for someone else, and if they do, they're in a very specific "visioning" role. Conceivers are not interested in small details and can sometimes be known for all talk and no action.

For entrepreneurs with an existing staff, it's a productive activity to have each team member take this test so roles and assignments are distributed correctly.

As an entrepreneur, you likely have a higher number, so when hiring, hire those with lower numbers; people who can listen well and work hard at assigned tasks. The higher your number, the lower the numbers of your staff should be. With a staff competent in detail, you'll be able to focus more on the big picture.

Generally, you are the visionary of your company, and your staff are the integrators. You're the dreamer, they're the doers.

Often, businesses are run by visionaries with high numbers. They scan the horizon for new opportunity, find new clients, and always think positively; it comes easy for them. **They don't over-think, they over-dream**; understanding waiting for perfect is never as smart as making progress. They dream, assign, and dream some more.

The most successful businesses have one visionary (known as the CEO, or chief executive officer), one main integrator (the COO, or chief operations officer), and then everyone else – like a pyramid.

The CEO develops ideas and the main integrator

gets those plans into action, serving as a conductor to "make sure the trains leave on time." If it's a large company, that main integrator sends trains to smaller stations (representing company departments) led by an integrator for that particular department (VP of Sales, VP of Marketing, VP of HR, etc).

Once your number has been thoroughly recognized, the second step in activating self-awareness is developing a **DISC Profile.** Now, before you roll your eyes thinking this is beginning to sound like a college textbook, stay tuned.

DISC stands for 'dominance, influence, steadiness, and conscientiousness.'

Decide which DISC type describes you best:

– **Dominance:** competitive, decisive, daring, adventurous, persistent, innovative
– **Influence:** charming, convincing, enthusiastic, optimistic, sociable, trusting, inspiring
– **Steadiness:** understanding, patient, good listener, stable, team player, relaxed, sincere
– **Conscientiousness:** precise, fact-finder, objective, accurate, detailed, courteous, compliant

Once you know your DISC style (and a friend or

two confirm your decision), look a little deeper:

– **If you're dominant,** you're generally concerned with being #1. You strive for results, you like having choices, you like change, you prefer to delegate, you want others to notice your accomplishments, and you need to be in charge.

– **If you're an influencer,** you're concerned with approval and appearances, you think emotionally, you like innovation, you often need help getting organized, you seek enthusiastic people, and you like feedback that you "look good."

– **If you're steady,** you want the facts, you're concerned with stability, you avoid risks, you dislike conflict, you enjoy team work, you want sincere feedback, you don't like change, and you enjoy calmness.

– **If you're conscientious,** you seek data, you need to know the process, you utilize caution, you prefer to do things yourself, you avoid conflict, and you enjoy when others notice your accuracy.

The DISC styles can grow even more condensed:

Your "openness" with others:
– **Dominance:** direct with thoughts, guarded with

emotions
- **Influence:** direct with thoughts, open with emotions
- **Steadiness**: indirect with thoughts, open with emotions
- **Conscientiousness:** indirect with thoughts, guarded with emotions

Your work–pace/business–style:
- **Dominance:** fast–paced, task–oriented
- **Influence:** fast–paced, people–oriented
- **Steadiness:** slow–paced, people–oriented
- **Conscientiousness:** slow–paced, task–oriented

Your fears:
- **Dominance:** being taken advantage of, lack of control
- **Influence:** being left out, loss of social approval
- **Steadiness:** sudden change, loss of stability and security
- **Conscientiousness:** being criticized, loss of accuracy and quality

Your weaknesses:
- **Dominance:** patience, sensitivity, looking at details, allowing for deliberation
- **Influence:** complete follow–through, speaking directly and candidly, researching all the facts
- **Steadiness:** adapting to change, multitasking,

confronting others
- **Conscientiousness:** delegating, compromising, making quick decisions

Knowing your style helps you tailor your management team to suit your weaknesses. More importantly, it allows you to evaluate where to improve yourself! With your Leadership IQ Number and DISC Profile, you have the clarity to know how to better yourself and your company.

Whether you're the most passive or intense by nature, know this: you have it in you to lead, to hold your crew accountable, and to hold yourself accountable. No matter what people may say about you, turn it around to motivate yourself. You are your OWN biggest cheerleader when it comes to your weaknesses.

Barbara Corcoran, *Shark Tank* millionaire, knows all about self-motivation. **"I grew up with dyslexia, and in school I was labeled the dumb kid. I spent my entire life trying to prove I'm not stupid, and that's the honest truth… that's what drives me,"** she shared. She took her weakness and made it her driving force into success.

Corcoran had another issue to overcome when her boyfriend ran off and married her secretary.

"You'll never succeed without me," he told Barbara. That drove her even faster into success. And based on her portfolio today, she's clearly 'arrived.'

Lori Greiner, another millionaire from *Shark Tank*, had a similar story. **"When I first started, there were several people – people I knew well – who just weren't believers... it lit a fire under me to prove them wrong. And they actually did me a favor because they made me stronger. I learned not to look back, but to look forward."**

Like the women mentioned above, there will be roadblocks, and saying 'YES' to your dreams mean saying 'no' to something else, often being predictability, professional comfort, and general ease.

However, despite the ups and downs of growing a company, it's an exhilarating ride few even attempt. Cultivating your strength–set defined above, there's a pilot somewhere in you. Keep your stick forward and fly over the pond; Amelia sure did. You'll find yourself landing in Ireland before you know it.

And the longer you wait for the future, the shorter it will be; now is the time. Everyone has the power to be an entrepreneur.

You don't need anyone's permission. Live like Richie; pack up and go.

Chapter Five:

Poppin' My Colla'

"I never went to fashion school. I didn't know what a designer was. (But) I knew I had something."
– Ralph Lauren

"Just look how slick that guy is, Jerry. Look at that suit!"

Ralph wasn't one to stay quiet during movies, and throughout this particular film, he was louder than usual, whispering to his brother with every new scene.

Mesmerized by actor Cary Grant's demeanor and wardrobe, Ralph dreamed of the day he'd be that polished.

The young Ralph, having grown up with immigrant parents and four siblings in a Jewish borough of

New York City, wasn't handed a silver platter upon birth. In fact, he was handed a horrendous last name instead: "Lifshitz," in which he was mercilessly teased day in and out at school.

While the refined Cary Grant turned heads, Ralph often felt just the opposite: overwhelmingly ordinary.

As the two brothers left the movie theater and made their way back home, they took in the busy, crowded streets of the Bronx; the ones they had grown accustomed to throughout their lives.

Shortcutting through narrow alleys they could practically navigate blindfolded, Ralph spoke up again.

"You know, Jerry, we don't have to live like this. We can do anything we want with our future. We could change our last name, even travel the world! There's so much to see out there, Jerry!"

Eyes on his shoes, hopping over a bag of trash, Ralph's brother chuckled to himself, having grown accustomed to hearing these inspirational schemes. However, he did happen to agree on the name change part.

With a few steps in thought, Ralph's brother finally responded. "I don't know about all that, but, you know Ralph... I think a name change could do us some good."

Eyes wide as saucers accompanied with a shout louder than a local at a Mets game, Ralph felt enlivened, recognizing a new name meant a new start.

And by the looks of it, it was. Deciding between a few different ideas, determined to sound as American as possible, the duo chose 'Lauren,' and it was official.

The name change, finished in a matter of weeks, lit something inside Ralph. He saw it as the first step toward starting a new life; a life of luxury, class, and channeling his inner Cary Grant.

He yearned – no, craved – a life of both influence and affluence. He'd had enough of borough living, and he wanted to start something fresh.

Mulling over the sleekness of Cary Grant and similar figures of prominence, Lauren harbored an innate fascination with crafting his persona, and he had a particular gift when it came to external drapery.

Naturally fascinated in menswear, Lauren developed a keen sense on the science of combining preppy and vintage looks, for both himself *and* others.

Accepting a sales position at Brooks Brothers, a high-end menswear designer, Lauren quickly became a top salesman with the brand, discovering his natural ability to style men based on their body type and preferences. High-class executives from all over New York, Wall Street specifically, began flocking to Lauren in droves.

An entrepreneur by nature, he wasn't blind to his talent, figuring the Brooks Brothers didn't want to add an extra brother to their ownership union. Thus, working late into the night, Lauren kept busy developing his own brand of wide-cut, bright neckties, quite unique compared to anything in the market.

Titling his brand 'Polo' — the horseback sport of elitists — Lauren planned to market his ties as the "classy, yet approachable" alternative.

Large department stores, including big-time Bloomingdales, caught wind of Lauren's talent and, to his sheer delight, picked up the Polo neckties, intrigued by the name and style. Concerned as Lauren was about sales, the ties quickly sold out and orders piled through the roof.

Acquiring a $30,000 loan, Lauren retired his hustling at Brooks Brothers and quickly blueprinted a full menswear line, shortly followed by womenswear.

Following smashing success, Lauren hit the big-time with one, simple, signature item: collared, short-sleeved cotton shirts available in 24 colors. Elevating the top-shelf of the universal fashion world with no formal training, Lauren, just 32, had become a phenomenon overnight.

Asked to outfit the cast of 'The Great Gatsby' in 1974, Lauren, flattered, mentally commemorated inhaling the posh Cary Grant films as a young man. He recollected life as a teenage Jewish boy with an unfortunate last name, possessing no cash in his pocket or suits in his closet.

He remembered hoping – wishing – he could someday understand the inner workings on demeanor and class. His hopes adapting to reality, he became, arguably, the classiest man in the world. Lauren morphed from an average young man into an uber-billionaire, broadening his luxury clothing line into home–furnishings, luggage, watches, eyewear, fragrances, shoes, and children's clothes.

From designing the Team USA Olympic uniforms to marrying the niece of an American President, Lauren built a name for himself, a name titling his $10 billion dollar enterprise. More importantly, he built a kingdom out of mere dreams and raw talent.

"People ask how a Jewish kid from the Bronx can do preppy clothes. Does it have to do with class and money? No, it has to do with dreams," Lauren's shared.

While Lauren's story may sound too exceptional to be relatable, there is much to learn from his journey. His success, in a nutshell, is due to one simple trait: **he knew his target customer.**

Representing the British gentry and American upper–class, all Polo products were and are tailored, generally speaking, with a preppy, aristocratic spin. Working at Brooks Brothers, Lauren spotted a gap in the market to appease the that particular community.

Like Polo, every company tailors their services and

products toward a unique people–group, whether consciously or not. What many companies fail to do, however, is develop that 'target customer' early.

No business can be all things to all people. Defining a 'target customer' (or 'target market') serves as the first component in developing a brand and marketing strategy. If the target customer is unknown, there is seemingly no possible way to tailor marketing efforts correctly.

Developing a target customer is as simple as pie. I'll show you!

Slice one is classifying the general client:

• Businesses (known as B2B – business to business)
• Consumers (known as B2C – business to consumer)

The two divisions are pretty self–explanatory. If you want to sell donuts, your market is 'consumers.' If you want to sell donuts with business logos stamped on them, your market is 'businesses.' Consumers are normal, everyday people. Businesses are, well, businesses.

Slice two is concluding what your 'field,' or general profession, is. Examples of 'field' types are 'Finance,' 'Business,' 'Retail,' 'Hospitality,' etc. Your company field is your broad profession type, and determining this is rather simple.

Slice three is pinpointing your 'niche,' or specific clientele focus. This is determined through defining characteristics about your 'perfect customer' and takes a bit more effort.

Your perfect customer, broken down, can their include gender, age, ethnic background, income, occupation, education, household size, religion, generation, nationality and even social class. The clearer the niche, the more effective marketing and services become.

Creating the niche is where many businesses fail. They never hone in on their focus, and their services/marketing efforts suffer.

When all three slices (business type, field, niche) are clear, the brand has room to thrive with no question marks. Here's an example:

Clothing–chain Lane Bryant is a **B2C** organization. The **field** is retail. And their **niche** is providing designer–like clothing, lingerie, and shoes to plus–

size, fashion–forward women in the United States.

They know their focus; hence, they succeed.

Creating a niche distinguishes a company. **Toyota has a different target market than Rolls Royce, and Aldi has a different target market than Whole Foods.** Developing the niche is like planting the business seed. Product/service development, pricing, quality, and advertising all sprout as branches from that single seed.

The more specific the niche, the better. Some companies go so far as to create a fictional background about their ideal customer. Take a candy shop for example: "Our ideal customer is named John, he's 17–years–old, walks home from school, loves bazooka bubble gum, comes from a middle–class home, and works at Jimmy Johns." They would be a B2C candy shop which focuses on average passerby's.

A different candy shop could take an entirely different route: "Our ideal customer is a multi–million dollar business who attends trade–shows on weekends and wants something unique to give attendees with their logo stamped on the packaging of candy." This would be a B2B candy shop which focuses on corporations.

Let's dive a little deeper, shall we?

Characterizing Your 'Niche' 101:

1. Create a wish list — Those who try to do business with everyone end up confusing the public about their brand. Once you've accepted how 'no business does business with everybody,' your mind will be malleable.

Let's be practical, here. Ask yourself the following: **"What types of people do I aspire to do business with? Who do I want calling my company, promoting my brand, and using my product/ service? Who, deep down, do I aspire to serve? Who are 'my people?'"**

Take an I.T. company, for example. Answering "anyone with I.T. needs" doesn't cut it, it's too broad. "National non–profits who receive over $1 million in donations in need of email, server storage, and maintenance," on the other hand, is a clearer target.

Getting as specific as possible is the goal with the wish–list; down to age, geographic location, gender, and socio–economic status.

Without knowing your 'dream customer,' you'll confuse the market by trying to do business with everybody. This leads to you feeling overworked, accompanied with a world wondering if they belong with your brand or not.

2. Focus — Zero in on what you want to sell, keeping in mind how in the beginning, "smaller is bigger."

Lauren launched Polo strictly selling neckties to executive men, then from there branched out once he'd proven himself in that solo arena.

Entrepreneurs often give away the entire kitchen – plus the kitchen sink – when opening. This muffles the brand, and consumers don't get excited for a muffled brand. Don't despise the day of humble, niche-based beginnings!

3. Pursue your talents — Often, we forget about our naturally given, innate skills because we, as humans, think we always need to take the harder, or "smarter," road. Business-mapping is not the time to do that!

Your company niche can arise based off your history. For example, if you spent six years working at a high-end restaurant and another ten working at an accounting firm, you could open an accounting service that focuses on high-end restaurants. Use your background as a compass!

4. Get in your customer's shoes — The best way for both new and existing companies to understand the worldview of their niche is as simple (and free) as talking to the perceived customer-base and discovering their concerns. Then, figure out how to heal those concerns.

Jimmy Johns, for example, heals the concerns of their customers. Jimmy Johns is known for their "freaky fast" sandwich making and delivery, and their niche is serving people on a time-crunch.

They do it, too. **Jimmy Johns is 3x faster than Subway at making sandwiches because of the process.** While Subway has customers choose each of their individual items, starting with the size, then bread, meat, veggies, and dressing, Jimmy Johns does all that FOR the customer.

All sandwiches at Jimmy Johns come the same: lettuce, tomato, onion, and they're all 8-inches. So, while a Jimmy John's customer orders a "#4, no onion," a Subway customer is still contemplating the 12-inch over the 6-inch. And then they have to choose all their meats, toppings, dressing, and whether they want it toasted!

This is not to bash Subway, as their motto is "healthy and fresh," and they're arguably healthier than Jimmy Johns, meaning both brands stick closely to their niche.

Finding a niche and creating a product and process that follows suit is crucial to building the perfect sandwich, a.k.a. your company!

5. Be open to molding — Business leaders tend to plug their ears at the suggestion of change, but (beneficial) adjustments separate the good from great.

For example, coffee powerhouse Starbucks recently decided to forego straws in place of sippy–cups to better the environment. By rewriting their business model, they remain relevant and 'cutting edge.'

Another brand, Coca Cola, had to adjust an advertising strategy for greater relevance. In 2014, Coke began stamping names of people on their bottles. After realizing they missed an opportunity, they reformatted the strategy. Rather than simply stating a name, they stamped "Share a Coke with…(name)." Now, instead of their target customer just being a 'Veronica,' it became 'Veronica and all the friends who could buy it for her.'

Be Strategic With Your Brand

A brand should allow for malleability and welcome change, creating a 'one of a kind' feel that stands out in the market. There is always a better, easier way to grow a profit. As author H. Brown stated, "don't be afraid to go out on a limb, that's where the fruit is!"

By understanding your business type, field, and niche, your 'perfect customers' will be lining up at the door. Craft wisely, and you may just find yourself 'popping collars' at the top of your industry with Ralph!

Chapter Six:

Planes, Trains & Ambulances

"It's kind of fun to do the impossible."
– Walt Disney

"Walter! Your schoolwork... remember? School comes before those silly paintings! Don't you want to be successful like your brothers?"

Following a long silence, a meek "yes, mum" emerged from the drawing room. Walter, an art–consumed 10–year–old, grumbled a "hmph," slowly standing to grab a math book from the shelf.

The young boy had grown accustomed to hearing about 'school this, school that' from his mum and pa, whom immigrated to the states and worked for every penny they had. His parents expected their five children to 'follow the system' as they did. Four took to it, but young Walter was a different breed altogether.

"Mum, I don't think I'm cut out for this school stuff, I really don't. My friends have a favorite subject... but me, I... I don't have a single one..." the boy whimpered, glancing again at his half-finished painting.

Walking into the room, a warm smile on her face and fruit juice in hand, his mother sighed and handed him the cup. Crouching down with a smile, she offered her encouragement.

"Someday, sweetie, you'll learn to love math, science, and even history. You'll just learn to love them in your own little way," she answered in a soft, calming tone, squeezing his shoulder.

Nodding slowly with a half smile, he accepted a forehead kiss, sipped the juice, and began ironing out a fraction.

As the months ticked by and Walter tried his best to feel somewhat interested in his schoolwork, his parents suggested a rather lovely idea to spark his passion for education: travel.

Walter's Uncle Mike, a train conductor, agreed to allow his nephew to tag along on a few treks, of which the boy quickly agreed to.

Pleased with the trips, Walter loved how his hair blew in the wind outside the caboose, how he could see open land for miles, and how the loud "toot, toot" of the whistle blasted when they reached a crossing.

Young Walter became mesmerized by the whole lifestyle, and learning the math, science, and history of locomotives accompanied that passion. Realizing his mother had been right, he saw first-hand how he could love any subject; he just needed to love them his own way.

Advancing into a bushy-tailed, chipper young man, the world was unfortunately operating just the opposite. Horror stories bleeding from the radio illustrating the ongoing World War, Walter felt a forceful pull.

An able-bodied sixteen years of age, he knew he wasn't old enough to serve in the military. But he ached to do something, anything, to help.

Leaving his expanding education behind, dropping both the heart of his un-approving mother as well as out of school, Walter enlisted. Turned down by the armed forces, he was convinced he'd weasel his way into service one way or another.

Reaching out to multiple organizations, a forged birth certificate in hand, Walter finally found his break. Reluctant but willing, the Peace Corps signed the youthful Walter as an ambulance driver.

Arriving in France lively and spirited, Walter immediately witnessed unthinkable horror, with screams shrieked directly in his ear on a minute-to-minute basis. Exposed to insurmountable terror, he (as if to cope with the distress) made himself a promise.

No matter what, he would not waste his talents, life, or time. Instead, he'd spend his bodily resources constructing the OPPOSITE of terror — JOY — for the world, a world so clearly broken with discord.

Witnessing enough turmoil for a lifetime, he vowed to reverse frowns to smiles and tears to laughter upon his return to the states.

After his two years overseas, of which he somehow survived by visualizing himself riding an open-aired caboose instead of his gut-wrenching ambulance, he fulfilled his committed duty. Stepping afoot back on American ground, the portal through which to execute his promise became obvious. He would use his natural gifting, the one that led to trouble too often as a lad — art.

Pondering the early conversations with his mother, he remembered how artistry was his first love. It being his passion, he knew he'd have no trouble using it as a vehicle, much like an ambulance, to drive the hurting toward ease.

Venturing to forge the unconventional, he recalled how telegrams were sent from France to the states informing families of the dismal news regarding their loved one's passing. So, he chanced to create a new, positive spin on the word. He launched "Laugh-O-Grams," seven-minute mini-films featuring cartoons. They were an immediate success to his home-based Kansas City crowds.

Deciding to take his skills to the next level, Walter, along with his brother Roy, pooled their money together and moved to Hollywood. And thanks to this leap to La-La Land, a metaphorical 'war zone to the top' of its own, Walter was offered his big break, all with just one, simple cartoon character.

Big round ears, floppy shoes too big for his feet, and a button nose, the smiling cartoon had a name soon evoking smiles across the country: Mickey Mouse.

Producing multiple short, silent films with Mickey, Walter struck gold with his first sound–flick, "Steamboat Willie." An instant sensation, Walter began pounding out films left and right to keep up with demand.

Creating Micky's friends of Minnie Mouse, Donald Duck, Goofy, and Pluto, the "Mickey Mouse Club" served as a beacon of light throughout the Great Depression.

Walter, now with a growing team and blueprints for a Burbank studio, expanded from just Mickey and created the first ever full–length animated film: "Snow White and the Seven Dwarfs," grossing an unimaginable $1.49 million, winning a total of eight Oscars.

Pinocchio, Fantasia, Dumbo, Bambi, Cinderella, Treasure Island, Alice in Wonderland, Peter Pan, Lady and the Tramp, Sleeping Beauty, and 101 Dalmatians were right on Snow White's tail, and in all, over one–hundred features were produced in the studio under Walter.

Finally deciding to produce not just movies, but memories, Disney made his 'finale' one to remember.

Purchasing a massive plot of land near Los Angeles, he built what he claimed was the 'Happiest Place on Earth:' **Disneyland**, complete with, of course, a rideable train.

Then–actor Ronald Reagan at Walter's side opening day, the park bustled, quickly increasing his initial investment ten–fold. And shortly after his career's pinnacle, Disney passed and was laid to rest at the age of sixty–five.

Disney's legacy, however, kept right on moving. Within a few short years, parks in Orlando, Tokyo, Paris, and Hong Kong were added to the franchise, along with hundreds of films creating worldwide laughter from millions, young and old.

For many even today, the long–term success of the Disney Franchise is a mystery. Many wonder how, decades after the passing of Walter, the mission and success didn't pass, too.

However, with a single visit to Disneyland any

moment of any day, the questions fade. By simply meeting any employee, janitor to Mickey himself, skeptics can't help but smile.

The reason for this contagious joy is **strategic**, not happenstance. When the Disney park organization has a new hire, their first order of business is resolute: be and act HAPPY, or else you don't belong.

Walter was famous for explaining how **"there is no magic in magic, it's instead all in the details."** When he opened Disneyland, he wanted to focus on those details to create that magic.

Walter wanted every interaction with every visitor to serve as a chance to shine, and he called these interactions "moments of truth." Each interaction was an opportunity to create a positive impression that could last a lifetime.

Because of this fierce determination to create magical moments, Disney is deemed the most customer-centric company in the entire world, earning customers, and entire families, for life.

Walt Disney's invaluable formula for brilliance is instilled from the top executives all the way to the part-time cleaning crew, with each employee referred to as a "cast-member." Disney wants every park guest to feel they're walking into a "show" when they enter Disney World, and that THEY are in fact the star.

Walter knew show-business, and he realized by perfecting the art of customer relations, he could transfer that into his California fairy-tale world, sparking customer loyalty, satisfaction, and legendary repeat business.

Like Disney, every company produces a "show" of some sort for their customers. That show determines whether or not those customers return.

Author Seth Godin agrees companies must be set-apart in order to be noticed and returned to: **"In a crowded marketplace, fitting in is a failure. In a busy marketplace, not standing out is the same as being invisible,"** he explains.

Godin describes in his book *Purple Cow* how, on a vacation in France, he understood this principle. Driving along the countryside with cows everywhere, he saw farms, winding hills, pastures – cows, cows, cows. But out of nowhere, and in a bit of a daze, Godin had a thought.

"You know what would make one of these cows stand out? If it were bright purple."

He goes on to explain: "Cows, after you've seen them awhile, are boring. They may be perfect cows, attractive cows, cows with great personalities... but they're still boring. A purple cow, though. Now that would be interesting."

The point Godin made is simple – **if a branding strategy isn't remarkable; if it doesn't turn heads or surprise the market or put on a worthwhile "show," then it's another black-and-white moo-moo cow on the hills of France, chomping on grass with the other thousands of cows in the pasture.**

When something is new, interesting, and exceptional, it's worth talking about. It's not invisible. Godin finishes his argument with a beautifully accurate recommendation: to stop advertising and start innovating.

Although there's no magic formula for breaking into the market with the loudest "MOO," there is one important tactic to help businesses get ahead: the art of constructing the perfect mission statement.

Creating a loyal following and becoming a "purple cow" begins with creating a mission statement that clearly encompasses the direction the company plans to go. It's broad enough to serve as the roadmap for years to come (including potential roadblocks or detours), but focused enough the general direction is obvious.

The Walt Disney Company, for example, boasts this as its mission: "we seek to develop the **most creative, innovative and profitable entertainment experiences** and related products in the world." It's broad, yet clear.

When writing a mission, consider the following:

– Why are you in business?
– Who is your customer base?
– What level of service do you provide?
– How do you differ from the market?
– What underlying values do you portray in your business?
– What are the goals of your business?

Setting aside time to physically write out these answers can help craft the who, why, and how of your mission and overall direction. Some mission statements are short (i.e. Starbucks: "To inspire and nurture the human spirit — one person, cup and neighborhood at a time") and some are long (i.e. beauty company Drybar listed ten core values with examples in place of a typical mission statement).

A unique way to craft a set-apart mission? Pizazz. Using offbeat words or phrases, like "spunky, outrageous, marvel, zest, sizzle," along with colorful phrases, can set your company apart from the market in a day and age when fitting in is the fastest road to mediocrity.

Once you've brainstormed, bounced ideas around with your team, and finally nailed down a mission between two and two-hundred words, get the word out. Print and post it all around your office so your employees can see it, get it on your website, and even consider attaching it to your email signature.

Make sure you learn it, live it, and actually achieve it, because 75% of employees don't think their mission is the way the company actually does business. **Walk what you talk.**

Facebook founder Mark Zuckerberg did just that. In 2006, after interviewing CEOs from Microsoft, Apple, and others to get a sense of how to develop a strong culture, **he was strongly advised** to write a succinct list of what it would mean to work at Facebook.

Here is the list Zuckerberg developed over ten years ago **describing his 'perfect employee' at Facebook:**

– Very high IQ
– Strong sense of purpose
– Relentless focus on success
– Aggressive and competitive
– High quality bar, bordering on perfectionism
– Likes changing and disrupting things
– New ideas on how to do things better
– High integrity
– Surrounds themselves with good people
– Wants to grow real value over perceived value

Mark took that list and placed it in a drawer. Three years later, the list was found, and employees were floored with how "on point" the list was as well as how it embodied Mark himself to a tee.

80% of a company's culture is determined by its core leaders; they're the ones who launch the company into a specific direction. Mark knew early what type of company he wanted to lead, and that initial description helped create a powerful culture.

Molly Graham, a Facebook employee who found the list, described it this way: "A founder saying something is like throwing a rock into a pond and watching the ripples. People immediately start repeating it. **At Facebook, Mark would say something and the next day it would be on the walls."**

There's no doubt the talented Facebook minions (I mean, employees) embody each of the traits listed by Mark, and because the Harvard-bred Mark hired men and women similar to himself and his strict beliefs, Facebook flourished.

In addition to Facebook building a prosperous interior culture, it built a favorable public culture, too. Facebook understands how consumers (especially millennials) are drawn to organizations that care, so the social platform decided to brilliantly add small touches to the general framework.

For example, when users log-in, Facebook often welcomes the viewer with a greeting: "Good morning, (insert name here)! Hope you have a great day!"

Facebook not only provides an avenue to connect with friends online, but it now is turning into a friend itself for its users.

These small touches add up to genius marketing that keep users on the website for hours a day – so much so, it's been studied **people can grow as dependent on Facebook as hard drugs, which is exactly how Facebook likes it.** Facebook becomes the friend of choice when a (non–digital) friend isn't available.

Another company who broke into the market with a booming "MOO" is the canned sparkling water company 'Bubly.' Having emerged into the public eye swiftly – perhaps quicker than Facebook – the fizzy water executives knew they needed an edge to compete with powerhouse LaCroix.

Although their aluminum can design isn't any more "purple" than LaCroix, there is one small detail that doesn't go unnoticed: they stamped a greeting – "hiiii," "oh hi," "yo," "hiya," "heyo," or "haaay" – on the lid of each of their cans, as if their beverage was less of a drink and more an old friend.

Even when consumers forget about seeing the greeting, this branding technique instantly flips a subconscious switch so they'll be more inclined to choose Bubly at the grocery store. Bubly is building brand loyalty amongst consumers who once swore total allegiance to LaCroix because they understand effective marketing.

Another company employing unique marketing is Bud Light, and you're likely familiar with the campaign. Let me give you a hint: it's a phrase, two identical words, and they mean absolutely nothing. Dilly, dilly.

The "dilly, dilly" campaign was created by an advertising agency named Wieden+Kennedy, and when the man in charge of the campaign, Miguel Patricio, was asked for his take on it, his response was comical.

"To tell you the truth, we never expected this to be so successful! It didn't test that well... but we hoped consumers would get it."

When asked what there was to 'get,' Patricio's response was even more humorous: "'Dilly Dilly' doesn't mean anything. That's the beauty of it. I think we all need our moments of nonsense and fun. And I think that "Dilly Dilly," in a way, represents that."

Patricio went on to explain the day the campaign had officially "made it." Typing "Dilly, dilly" into Amazon, he found ten different companies selling t-shirts with the slogan. When asked whether he'd be suing those companies over copyright, he said "no, no… we want everybody to "Dilly Dilly" in their life, so no problem at all!"

Once a campaign "goes viral," it sells itself. The odd, yet light-hearted Bud Light campaign worked, proving just how 'out-of-the-box' brands must go with marketing nowadays to gain major recognition.

On some occasions, however, certain out-of-the-box thinking may be unhealthy for the company. An example of this is Taco Bell's famous chihuahua, Gidgit.

Gidgit was first introduced to the public via television in 1997, using the famous phrase "Yo quiero Taco Bell," meaning, of course, "I want Taco Bell."

The Taco Bell campaign was popular. So popular, chihuahua sales around the country rose tremendously, and the Chihuahua Club of America was overjoyed by the response. The problem with the campaign, though, is albeit its popularity, it didn't drive up Taco Bell's sales. In fact, sales dropped.

People thought the dog was cute, but they didn't like associating dogs with their food. Dogs and tacos didn't mix as well as Taco Bell hoped it would have, and eventually, in 2004, the company dismissed the campaign. They found themselves selling dogs, not tacos (the Chihuahua Club of America even begged Taco Bell not to stop, so Taco Bell decided to continue selling the stuffed animal Gidget online to appease the organization).

Choosing a "purple cow" branding campaign is important, but it also has to work!

A company named Unilever gets this. A major player in the personal hygiene sector, Unilever owns 'Dove' and 'AXE.'

Funny part is, although these two brands are owned by the same company, their messaging is quite different. Dove's message is themed as 'womanly, kind, and heart-driven,' while the history of AXE's messages are generally 'masculine, tough, and sex-driven.'

Dove has three main commercials that went viral:
– **Beauty Sketches**: presenting the problems with

how women perceive themselves
- **Revolution**: portraying how makeup/photoshop skews real-life
- **Beauty Pressure**: presenting how young girls get unhealthily bombarded with beauty ads

They all have the same message to customers, which Dove explains on their website: **Dove helps girls build body confidence and self-esteem.**

Unilever owns AXE, too. It's the same type of product as Dove – body wash, soaps, skin care – but for men.

Unilever wanted to capture emotions of men the same way Dove captured the emotions of women, only they did the opposite way. In fact, it can be (strongly) argued AXE's branding actually undermines everything Dove tries to promote.

One such Axe commercial is titled "Billions." In this commercial, countless stick-thin beauty models in skimpy bikinis are running through a jungle toward a man spraying AXE on himself. The commercial text reads "Spray more. Get More."

Very peculiar, isn't it, how a company can boast the importance of inner beauty with one brand and hire hundreds of half-naked models for another brand? **In a sense, the AXE commercials actually sell more for Dove, since AXE commercials hurt confidence of women and Dove serves as a gateway to pull it back up.**

Unilever, as inconsistent as their brands may be, is actually smart to do this. They play with emotions, and because of that, both brands are wildly successful with their campaigns. They know their "perfect customer" and advertise accordingly.

In fact, that's what all smart companies do. They create an imaginary "perfect customer," from the character's gender to age to marital status to income to interests. Dove knew (most) women feel some sense of unhealthy comparison, so they play on "inner beauty." AXE knew (most) men want to be attractive to the opposite sex, so they play on "amping masculinity."

The names and packaging alone drives sales from their "perfect customer." The term 'axe' refers to a strong man's tool, and the products are contained in black–as–night bottles with rough edges. The term 'dove' refers to a white bird representing peace and purity for women, and these products are contained in white, soft bottles with rounded edges. They know their customer!

McDonalds, the most successful burger–joint in all the globe, similarly understands their "perfect customer" to a tee.

For example, their 'kids menu' is not called simply the 'kids menu.' Instead, they chose a catchy name: 'Happy Meal.'

'Happy' is an easy word all toddlers learn to associate with joy. And since children are easy to please (or manipulate, rather) through simplistic messages, McDonalds knew it would work like a charm.

Happy Meals come in a special box (portraying them as a present), with a toy (associating the meal with play), and get delivered (on TV) by a red and yellow clown named Ronald. McDonalds understood the principle of attracting children and families so well, they built jungle gyms inside many of their locations. They were not just creating a restaurant – but a family destination.

Even adults get lured by their messaging. Just this morning, as I was driving past a pair of golden arches, the outdoor screen read "A GOOD DAY STARTS HERE," along with a giant cartoon smile. McDonalds plays into emotions using subliminal messages – we all want good days, and we all want to smile.

Their longtime jingle "bah–da–bum–bah–bah, I'm lovin' it" rings true for many. We're 'lovin it' and we literally 'eat up' the subliminal messages for breakfast, lunch, and dinner.

The best brands generate effective messages to the public sphere. They know their perfect client, they've studied what makes that client tick and what makes them smile, and they use said information to win the client. Long–term companies become as much like a "purple cow" as they can, developing a culture that attracts the right customer.

Disney creates magic, Facebook creates community, Bubly creates a liquid friend, Bud Light creates silliness, Dove creates inner beauty, AXE creates attractive men, and McDonalds creates happiness.

What will **your** branding create?

Chapter Seven:

He's Toast

"Advertising is the 'wonder' in Wonder Bread."
– Jef I. Richards

It was a warm day in 1912, warmer than most Missouri spring days, and the town jeweler, Otto, was running late again.

Finishing his brisk walk to the front door of one of his boutiques (his favorite of the three he owned and operated), he whistled loud as a tin flute while fumbling through his pocket for the right set of keys.

Sliding the key through the lock, he noticed there was a customer already waiting to enter, the little old woman from down the road with the not–so–little bank account.

Greeting her with a smile, nod, and a clearing of his throat, he beckoned her into the store, to which she clearly made known her frustration for his lack of timeliness.

Apologizing and still managing to sell her one of his latest collection pieces, he finally took the time to set down his bag, which had been slung over his shoulder throughout the schmoozing and transaction.

Realizing he'd probably have to face the facts and, at some point, figure out how to craft his schedule for less tardiness and greater efficiency, the underground craftsman and self–proclaimed 'fixer–upper' mentally played out his morning routine. Scanning his mind for time–squandering culprits, he fixated on one morning staple: packing his lunch.

Otto packed a lunch each dawn; a sandwich, usually. He'd slice a few pieces of turkey or ham from the previous night's leftovers, accompanying it with two slices of bread freshly cut from a bakers loaf — white or rye, generally.

Taking his cloth–wrapped sandwich out of his knapsack, he stared at it, contemplating his thoughts a little deeper. "Maybe... maybe there's a way to make lunch–packing quicker?," Otto pondered, looking at the sandwich a bit too long.

Plucking the bread off his sliced ham, he questioned why sandwiches, a fundamental lunchtime demand, weren't simpler to make.

Remembering how he'd meticulously cut two slices of rye from a fresh loaf in his pantry that morning, he wondered why he couldn't simply buy the bread that way. I mean, if Campbells Soup could can their chowder and Hershey Chocolate could wrap their kisses, surely someone could sell bread by the slice, right?

And if it didn't exist, well — why not? How difficult could it be? Henry Ford created a drive–able car, for goodness sakes, so surely someone could create a simple bread–cutter. Why wasn't that a thing?

Within moments, he heard the bell attached to his swinging door "ding!" as another customer walked in; a giddy, young man escorting pretty arm candy by his side. With a day busy as any other, Otto – who could be forgetful at times – allowed his newfound inventive–prowess to fall flat as a crushed ruby.

As the years passed by, the idea stagnantly stayed put in Otto's self-conscious. Strolling into the same boutique one day, late, due again to his tardiness — he decided he was done putting it off.

Unleashing his genius to friends, family, and customers regarding the invention and expecting encouragement, he received anything but. Instead, laughter was their response.

"Stick to your jewelry, Otto," he heard over and over. "You know everyone has a knife for cutting bread."

A little taken aback, yet not totally disheartened, he then approached the town bakers to explain the invention. The "experts" laughed just the same, convinced the sliced bread would literally fall apart if cut from a machine.

Otto, gaining nothing more than a faint heart and a few warm pastries the bakers had boxed him, knew there was more to his concept than laughs and criticism. Simple and supposedly problematic as it sounded, it was possible. Anything was, right?

Following his gut, he ignored them.

"I may be no Thomas Edison, but heck — I can be anything I want, inventor and all. I'll just believe in myself enough for the whole state of Missour–uh," Otto reflected, alleviating his dissipating optimism.

So, after months tinkering in his back office and drawing up the blueprints, Otto knew he was close. The decade–long phenomenon he'd been toying with in his brain was almost a reality.

However, Mother Nature had her venomous words to snarl about the invention, too.

After turning over his precious blueprints for a prototype to be built, the impossible happened: a factory fire ferociously seared the copy to a crisp.

Understandably feeling rather burnt himself, Otto found himself forced to either take it as a sign to quit like everyone suggested, or begin again.

And choosing the latter, he gave it one last shot.

Re–drawing the blueprints to cut loaves less than half an inch thick, he recreated the newfangled contraption and called it go–time. Lending the invention to his buddies' bread–baking company, the rest was history!

Well, almost, that is.

Otto now had sliced bread, along with his friends, some locals, and a few Midwestern foodies. It worked, he had done it, and he proved the doubters wrong!

Only problem was, no one else seemed to care. Otto's invention was smart as can be, but unfortunately, there was a missing ingredient: sharing his bread with the masses.

Selling only to a few supermarkets, it was a gold mine of an idea with no treasure map leading customers to the product.

So, to be expected, when a different company discovered Otto's invention, with its precise bread cuts and mammoth potential for customers, they jumped at the chance to replicate it.

The Taggart Baking Company took his same, coveted machine and did what Otto couldn't do: turn sliced bread into a world-wide phenomenon.

The Taggart executives knew they could take the machine Otto had worked tirelessly on and distribute sliced bread to every household in

America. They knew, with the right marketing and edge, they could launch the idea with massive success. All they needed was a legitimate "brand" to do it, a thought Otto ignored.

Elmer Cline, one of the company executives, developed the brand in a matter of seconds while enjoying the International Balloon Race at the Indianapolis Speedway. Witnessing a kaleidoscope of hundreds of balloons being released into the air, one word enveloped his mind: **wonder.**

And there he had it – Wonder Bread.

Wonder Bread took Otto's 10-year-old idea of sliced bread and spun it with creative advertising and marketing, including red, white, and blue balloons on the packaging and the tagline "building strong bodies 12 different ways."

The balloons presented the purchase as a celebration, and the tagline presented the purchase as a health tool; playing into the emotions of grocery-shopping housewives worldwide. Wonder Bread was the reason for the widely used phrase "the best thing since sliced bread," literally becoming a wonder to society.

The Wonder brand went on to create the coveted

Ding–Dongs and Twinkies, finding success for a full century after the launch. Wonder Bread knew exactly how to create a lasting brand through carefully crafting a 'story' around their products to engrave them into the lives of customers.

The secret to building success is – bottom line – innovation; to solve an impossible problem; to be exceptional, new, and interesting. Yet although Otto's sliced bread was innovative, no one knew about it. It wasn't marketed as a show–stopping product, proving no matter how genius an idea/ business may be – it will fall flat without the 'yeast' to grow its name.

Everything about Wonder Bread, however, was exciting and innovative to purchasers; down to the name.

Successful brands shift the status quo and literally get people to think differently. Wonder Bread took sliced bread and told people it would build strong bones, provide essential vitamins, and even make life a little easier with no knives required at lunch–time, all packaged in a friendly, balloon–covered parcel. What's not to like?

The Wonder brand thought outside the (bread) box with their brand. Otto, genius as his idea was, did not. Wonder realized there was a major opportunity available and jumped on it.

Robin Williams, in the *Dead Poet's Society*, explains the idea of thinking outside the norm: "I stand up on my desk to remind myself we must constantly look at things in a different way."

Although he wasn't referring to business, this principle deems true. Standing on 'hypothetical desks' allows for entrepreneurs to see a 'crack in the marketplace' to fill with their brand.

This can lead to a better product, brand, staff, or price than what's already out there, just like how the Taggart Company noticed a crack in the branding of sliced bread.

If there's a void in the market of any field of business and people would be willing to pay for that product/service, there's room to fill it with a company.

Instead of offering the same old thing hundreds of other companies offer, having a different spin attracts a sea of clients, making a brand invaluable.

If there's no void in the market, there's no major

business opportunity. Hence, before beginning a new professional venture, **it's crucial to identify if an untapped void in your industry even exists.**

Recognizing any legitimacy of a business idea depends on how the following questions are answered:

Who's the general demographic living in the area?
What would drive sales?
Where are you located in terms of competition?
When you analyze the local economy, is it a strategic economic time to open?
Why/how would you stand out from competition?

If any of these answers make you nervous, you'll have to find a new location, create a unique spin to your idea, or consider opening a different type of business altogether.

One of the most successful companies of our time, Facebook, which we talked about briefly in the last chapter, was built to fill a deep void. **The world wanted connection,** and Facebook became the new universal 'town square' to chat, sell, boast, flirt, and whine, creating that connection.

Facebook, or 'Facemash' as it was first named, was launched in a college dorm to rate the level of attractiveness of Harvard girls, soon shifting into an online connection point amongst the student body, expanding to Columbia, Stanford, and Yale. Facebook gradually opened to most universities in the United States and Canada, and in 2006, anyone over the age of 13 was valid.

We all know the rest: Facebook took over the world, employing over 20,000 Ivy-leaguer alumni, generating billions in annual profit, and boasting six new profiles every second. And it was all started in a dorm by an average sophomore filling a crack for a wide audience.

He understood the importance of filling a crack, and with a net worth of over $70 billion, he did pretty well. Currently, Zuckerberg only takes a salary of $1 a year from the technological monstrosity!

Zuckerberg found a crack. Yet, in a sense, finding a crack is the easy part. It's generally simple to think of a business idea or restaurant idea or product idea you wish existed in your area, whether online or brick and mortar. **The tough part is sticking to it long enough to execute the plan and become a valid entrepreneur.**

Growing a business, when visualized, is a lot like

walking to St. Louis (hang with me here).

St. Louis is 342.6 miles away from my desk right now. If I were to head outside and start walking south, I could easily go a mile, five miles, maybe even fifteen. I'd be excited, powered by thoughts of the fun I'd have — taking an Instagram photo in front of the arch and eating a hotdog at a Cardinals game. I'd walk along jolly as a Jolly Rancher whistling Judy Garland's *"Meet Me in St. Louis!"*

But give it a few hours, and I'd be over it. I'd want to take shortcuts, Uber, or just call it quits all–together.

Similarly, business owners grow weary trying to fill a crack. They run into problems monetizing their vision, throw their hands up, and yell "fuggetaboutit" ScarFace style, exactly why over 50% of businesses fold before the five year mark.

Many owners pull an 'Otto' by losing everything to Wonder Bread, failing to execute their brand correctly. Yet, the advice those who've "arrived" would tell you? "If you're passionate enough, don't quit. Corporate America will always be there if you fail. Another day, another step!"

There are **seven unique points every wise entrepreneur follows,** not only for the first fifteen miles, but for the end of the road, too. Let's dive in!

1. Just, simply, become the best:

Whatever your current brand philosophy may be, scrap it. Here's your new company–wide target: **make your product/service the best of its kind in the entire world.**

Instead of worrying about how to attract customers and make money, worry about the actual money–maker first.

An example is 'Jeni's Splendid Ice Cream.' Jeni Bauer, a former nurse with no business background prior to starting her parlor in 2002, had a mission to make the best ice cream in existence. She didn't know how she'd find customers, she just focused on developing and redeveloping her recipe until it was the best (many say, best in the world). Today, it's sold nationwide for a whopping $10 a pint at over 1,000 locations.

Their mission statement sums it up: "We believe (in) REALLY great ice cream served perfectly..."

The best ice cream in the world attracts the strongest fan base in the world. Becoming the best at your craft allows your empire to grow much easier than a dull product/service.

2. Competition is out there:

Standout basketball coach Michael Krzyzewski of Duke University (currently making over $8 million annually!) is known for his prized quote: **"Somewhere he is out there training while I am not. One day, when we meet, he will win,"** motivating his players to beat their metaphorical competitor.

When you realize there's always someone trying to beat you (or steal your customers, whether directly or indirectly), it keeps you on your toes for continuous development, correction, and reconstruction to be bigger, better, and more efficient.

If you want to be better than average, work harder than average. If you want to be the best, work harder than anyone.

To do that, wise leaders review and improve the process of their company often, including monitoring any overproduction, system downtime, underutilization of people, and excessive management.

One company has a unique platform to spark change: when an employee suggests a tactic to better the business, that employee receives the money saved from that change. Not just in their next paycheck, but forever. This opened the door for suggestions to be made in an open, friendly environment.

Find the root of any internal problems and correct the defects. Soon, instead of worrying about outworking your competition, you'll own your competition.

3. Hire mission–focused:

Online shoe giant Zappos has an excellent mission: "We deliver happiness to customers **and employees**." Zappos takes their hiring process and employee welfare seriously.

In order to attract the best, every Zappos employee must spend their first two weeks in extensive training to learn about the company's culture and mission. At the end of those two weeks, employees are given $4,000 and told to either keep the money and begin the job **or take**

the money and leave for good.

Zappos would rather employees leave prior to getting started before getting entrenched into the company if they're not 100% sold they can live up to the core values. And, hey, some leave with the money!

4. Be quick to listen, slow to speak:

The National Council of 4–H is the largest youth development program in the United States, and president Andy Ferrin is one busy bunny.

However, on top of her packed schedule, she manages to squeeze in time daily to sit in the massive campus cafeteria to eat lunch with her employees. Sitting with a different group every day, she asks about the "nitty gritty," learning first-hand of any office problems or insider knowledge on how to enhance the workplace experience.

She also instituted an employee suggestion box, reading each suggestion aloud at company meetings. One such suggestion read "our coffee is terrible." In response, she bought a new Keurig for every floor of the office building.

As a leader, learn to listen before the whispers turn to shouts.

5. Get (everyone's) hands dirty:

Motor manufacturer Honda doesn't like keeping their management in enclosed offices all year long, requiring every office-based employee to spend a week on the floor of the corresponding department they manage.

Office employees partake in the same jobs as those working in the factory. They wear the same clothes, and they stagger their weeks so all the office-workers aren't working the floor the same time.

This provides clerical staff members practical experience to know what the other employees are going through, establishing better practices in the overall process.

No need for "Undercover Boss" here!

6. Break down barriers:

At mid-to-large companies, cubicle barriers can keep staff departments isolated.

One advertising agency broke those barriers. The company stripped the interior building, including all their designated offices. Employees instead received a desk with wheels. Each room was deemed a different theme: a design room, quiet room, conference room, artistic room, and even a nap room.

Employees were encouraged to wheel their desks based on the project and the team they were working with. This company went so far, they even had buckets of paint in each room for employees to "paint their canvas" on the walls.

Project managers, designers, and programmers could therefore all wheel into one room for a certain project, then go their separate ways. I only wonder how full the nap room gets each afternoon...

7. Take the team 'back to school':

Back to Jeni's Ice Cream – each week, all employees have a "lunch and learn" where a different employee teaches something new that doesn't involve ice cream. One week, an employee will teach about rock climbing. The next, someone will teach on yoga, and on and on.

Regular education creates a mindset to continue learning. Instituting self–improvement keeps staff fulfilled and promotes out–of–the–box thinking.

Leading a session also grows the confidence of employees, building inevitable bonds of closeness amongst the team.

You've Got This

Otto failed to build a brand. You, however, now have the tools to fill a void, craft a brand, and keep on walking. Before you know it, you'll arrive.

Chapter Eight:

Undergrad < Hooters

"If you don't use your voice, there's someone
waiting behind you who will."
— Kate Cole, President of Focus Brands

"Can we get another order of wings over here,
sweetie?"

Kat sighed, ran to the kitchen, and asked the cook
for another order.

It was her fifth week on the job at Hooters. As a
high schooler with little experience (but not–so–
little dreams), she planned to use the job as a
means of saving for college.

Growing up in Jacksonville, Kat was surrounded
by wealth. Her friends at school wore the latest
designer clothes and purses, while Kat bought

everything on her own. With a single-mother who made a limited salary and three other siblings, Kat understood how she'd have to work her tail off to pay for school herself.

Working day and night, Kat did everything she could to save money and stand out. Serving overtime with a smile, she kept the Jacksonville Hooters in ship-shape. And with a die-hard will to make things happen for herself, she got noticed — even as a nineteen-year-old waitress.

After enrolling in the University of Florida and getting into a routine of work, class, and engineering homework, something happened Kat didn't anticipate.

Requested by her management to report to the national headquarters of Hooters in Atlanta, she was a bit shocked. She had no idea what they wanted, all she knew was she wanted to keep her job. Agreeing to go and making the five hour drive, she hoped for the best.

Upon arrival, she was quickly beckoned into an executive's office. "In here, Miss Cole!"

Nodding her head with as confident a smile as she could manage, she stepped into the office and took a seat.

"Kat, we've noticed your stand-out performance in Jacksonville," the man in the suit and tie started. "And we were wondering if you'd be willing to work as a Hooters ambassador, traveling the world to open new branches, getting them off on the right foot."

Mouth agape, quite unsure if she was dreaming or experiencing real-life, Kat stuck out her hand. "You've asked the right girl," she responded with a nod, knowing the offer was no-less than a golden ticket toward success.

Much to her mother's dismay, Kat dropped out of college to pursue the non-traditional path to prosperity. And at just nineteen, having never stepped foot on an airplane, Kat embarked on her first Hooters destination "down-under," Australia.

Kat's instincts proved correct, and she rose through the ladder quickly, accepting promotions regularly. By just twenty-six years old, she achieved the unimaginable, accepting her position as the Executive Vice President of Hooters, an unheard of concept for someone **without even a bachelor's degree.**

Yet Kat, being the trailblazer she was, had an idea to change that little detail.

She found it quite silly to have her prominent position void of a degree, so instead of starting from the bottom, Kat tried her hand at the unconventional: skipping her bachelors and applying straight for her masters. She knew, with the right recommendations, schools would be crazy not to accept her.

With recommendation letters from ten CEO's, one of which being Ted Turner (the founder of CNN), Kat stood out big-time.

Accepting her offer from the University of Georgia and walking into her first day of classes, Kat smiled to herself when asked where she'd received her undergrad. "Well... Hooters," she thought.

Kat's offbeat path up the ranks of the business world led to one opportunity after another, and at thirty-two, when most women were just securing their careers, Kat was offered the position of a lifetime: Presidency of Cinnabon, the sweet-smelling delicacy with 1,1000 stores in fifty-six countries.

Eventually offered an even higher position as Presidency of all the 'Focus Brand' entities (Cinnabon, Schlotzsky's, Moe's Southwest Grill, Auntie Anne's, Seattle's Best Coffee), she became, arguably, the most powerful woman in the service business.

Kat, today still young in the enterprise sphere at a mere forty, was, and is, not your typical entrepreneur. She worked hard enough to get noticed by the boss, wiping down tables at nineteen, and then she **became** the boss. She understood how opportunity came to those who stood out, doing just that.

"I was so thankful for my first job at Hooters, but I was grateful in moderation." Kat explained. "If you get too thankful for what you already have, it can hold you back from dreaming bigger. The key is to be thankful for things not being worse, but to never be afraid to work to make them better."

Kat manages men much older than she is due to her hard work as a teenage waitress. The principle of working hard and being a stellar waitress, or saleswoman – in a sense – is what set Kat apart in the business world.

And similarly, everyone selling something, from

$10 chicken wings at Hooters to a $100 million dollar home, can also use their personal selling ability to get a step ahead in the corporate world. We're **all** salesmen in our own right!

– We sell our parents on deserving an allowance.
– We sell our skill set to our future college.
– We sell ourselves on a date to our future spouse.
– We sell our resume to our first employer.
– We sell our bank on why we deserve a mortgage.

The reason for success in sales is simple: **make it seem as if you'd rather be the one receiving your "bargain" than selling it,** making your buyer feel special, as if they won big.

Let's break down how Mr. and Mrs. Smith, a hypothetical wealthy couple, spend their money:

– Mrs. Smith always shops for her jewelry at Tiffany's because "I feel so special working with the jeweler, Marco. He knows my style so well, and he always pours me a glass of champagne with each new purchase."

– Mr. Smith only buys his suits at Neiman Marcus because "Ken takes great care of me; if there's something I want they don't have, he'll get it tailor made for me and shipped directly to my house within a week."

– Mr. and Mrs. Smith enjoy dinner at a family–owned Italian restaurant on Madison Ave because "Chef Bonacelli knows our order by heart and still makes our favorite dish, even though it was taken off the menu. And they save the corner booth for us every Saturday night!"

This couple developed their favorites, and they stick to them. Similarly, in order to become a 'favorite' to the public, there's one crucial step to learn while selling: make it so you'd rather be the one buying than the one selling. Put yourself in the prospect's shoes.

The best word to use while selling a service or product is YOU. "YOU will benefit from this product/service because A, B, C."

A BMW salesman, for example, could convincingly and accurately use the word YOU to make a smooth sale using a variety of topics:

VALUE – "Since **YOU** drive to the beach everyday, this car is great for **YOU** because it'll be easy to clean out the sand. This model is perfect for

YOUR summer outings!"

FINANCES – "Because **YOU** just paid off your home loan, **YOUR** car payment plan for this vehicle would be the best for **YOU**. The monthly payments are perfect for **YOUR** budget."

COMFORT – "Take a seat, how do **YOU** feel? Relaxed, right? Since **YOU** just had shoulder surgery, the built–in massage feature could be great for **YOUR** long drives."

A successful seller once explained why he had the best job in the world: **"The salesman is the one who makes people's dreams come true. He helps them anticipate the future, turn today's visions into tomorrow's realities. He helps them fulfill their desires, satisfy their yearnings. He shows them how to become happier, healthier, more prosperous and secure, loved by their families, and respected by their friends."**

Only about 50% of small businesses make it to their fifth year, and building a committed client base is step one in not joining that dismal statistic. The majority of your sales will be (and should be) repeat customers, so taking care of clients well **the first time** will inevitably lead to repetition.

One standout salesman is billionaire Kevin O'Leary, or 'Mr. Wonderful' from CNBC's *Shark Tank*. With over five-hundred products generating north of $5 billion in sales, his resume commands attention.

Mr. Wonderful recently shared his tips on how to become a salesman of high-caliber.

Let's break down how Mr. Wonderful built his portfolio with his "Selling Secrets" below:

– "Create actual value"

The most successful entrepreneurs are the ones who created products/services with the most value. Selling something of low value may have momentary success in the short-term based on the initial hype, but after time goes on, the proof is in the pudding. Long-term success requires long-term value.

The two most successful organizations in the world today, Facebook and Google, provided significant value to the public before even making any money and running ads. They gained audience trust before running ads because they wanted to cultivate trust and value.

No value = dead company.

– "Help people"

If you're not improving anyone's life, you're wasting your time. A nice smile and practiced spiel can work for a period, but it takes a product that improves lives to catapult your business into long-term growth.

– "Don't be a 'Debbie Downer'"

We have over 60,000 thoughts a day, and it's our duty to keep those overwhelmingly positive. Think of a brain as a horse: it's running in a direction, and it's our job to steer it down the right road.

Not only are happy people, well, happier, but they sell more! **Optimistic salespeople sell 37% more than pessimists,** and they're 2x as likely to stay with a company over a year.

– "Bite the bullet and apologize"

Someday, if not already, you will get an angry client. Tilman Fertitta, billionaire owner of hospitality group Landry's, Inc, explained how he still has to say 'sorry' to customers every day!

Even with the most ludicrous of claims from upset customers where the complaint is not fully valid, **there's usually at least 1% of each complaint that is accurate.** Take each complaint seriously as a way to revamp your company.

– "Follow the 80/20 rule"

80% of business results are generated from 20% of the efforts. Within that 20%, there is another 80/20 rule, meaning a teeny–tiny amount of effort lead to the most results.

That small amount is exactly where you should focus your energy. It doesn't matter if you're working one–hundred hours a week if only ten of those hours lead to the major sales. Time is money!

Build Your Brand

Kat herself put it best, describing the importance of continual improvement: **"I ask the same two questions of the staff in every Cinnabon I visit: 'What do our guests ask for that we don't have?' and 'if you could, what would you change about this company?'"**

How can you, like Kat, create a more customer-centric company?

Chapter Nine:

...Netflix & Chill?

"Once you've hitchhiked across Africa with ten bucks in your pocket, starting a business doesn't seem too intimidating." — Reed Hastings, Founder of Netflix

"I'm in the exact place I'm supposed to be," Reed confidently whispered.

With the Boeing 747 halfway through its twenty-one hour journey, passenger Reed continued to mentally prepare.

"It'll be worth it, just wait and see," the college graduate told himself on repeat, fumbling in his backpack.

Asking the stewardess for yet another bag of chips as he flipped through his stack of math books, he let out a few deep breaths. Squinting out the window and seeing not in a cloud in the air, he knew he was making the right move.

Airborne toward Africa for two committed years in the Peace Corps, Reed planned to finish with some sort of clue where his life was taking him. Knowing he wanted to live for a greater purpose, he hadn't yet figured out the road. An adventure-haulic throughout college, and even serving a stint in the Marines, he knew his path would be anything but run-of-the-mill.

After a few more pep talks, black coffees, and attempts to nap, Reed groggily roused to the pilot on the intercom, "Welcome to the Kingdom of Swaziland – a royal experience!"

One last, deep breath, and Reed knew it was go-time.

Arriving to his new home and getting into the swing of his assignment teaching math to children, Reed was surprised how quickly he adapted to the Swazi lifestyle. And with the natural surroundings of his village being so beautiful, he felt rather cheerful fulfilling his committed days.

From the stunning landscapes of mountains,

forests, and plains, along with the wildlife reserves of lions, hippos, and elephants, Reed was a kid in a candy store, so to speak.

Feeling comfortable in the Swazi Kingdom provided the mental capacity to stretch himself throughout his two years calling Africa home. Practically no money in his pocket or plans on his 'off-work' schedule, he often hitchhiked to nearby countries, indulging in the obscure customs and relishing in local cuisine, people-groups, and exploration.

Having climbed countless mountains and made countless friends, the two years slowly trickled to one year, day, and minute. And after a full 730 days in the land of Swazi, he found himself just steps from his plane back West.

Leaving Swaziland – with all the joys and laughs and memories – Reed made himself a promise.

Using his African experience and all he'd learned about travel and teaching and the uncertainty of life, he vowed he'd forget worrying about his future. He promised he'd trust his instincts and make life one heck of an adventure, much like he'd done so far.

Mentally signing his name on his own contract and returning home to recondition himself to first-world living, Reed embarked on a kingdom entirely different than Swaziland: tech startups.

A keen young man, Reed sped through a masters degree in artificial intelligence (AI) from Stanford University, soon-after launching his own tech startup, Pure Software. Acquiring the ins and outs of leading not just a Swazi math class, but a full business, he learned to motivate, encourage, and teach in a business setting.

Although being a young chap, his instincts proved prodigious. Pure Software was so successful, it was soon acquired by another company for a whopping $750 million, ironically almost matching the amount of days he served in Africa. Dumbfounded by the booming profit, he remembered barely having enough money to eat whilst hitchhiking in Swaziland.

Cognizant of more talent he could endow to the world, Reed juggled business ideas to strategize his next move. Sure, he could easily hang his hat — yet something told him the best was yet to come.

Not waiting long, Reed received his answer

through a "golden ticket" of sorts, arriving without warning into his mailbox.

The gold, however, tinted itself as blue: it was a forty dollar late-fee from Blockbuster, accompanied with a notice scolding Reed for his overdue rental.

While only pocket change for the uber-millionaire, he grew perplexed.

"One late rental, probably costing ten bucks, and they have the audacity to charge four times the amount?," he mentally probed.

Heading to the gym after receiving the fee, he couldn't get the absurdity of the bill out of his mind. "I mean, even this gym has a better business model than Blockbuster! Pay forty bucks a month and exercise as little or as much as you want. Not per visit, or per movie! Why doesn't Blockbuster have a membership model, for goodness sakes?"

Stepping on a machine, he had his epiphany.

"That's it!" he sputtered, suddenly finding himself training harder than he had in weeks. He would create a more efficient, service-focused version of Blockbuster that was subscription-based, solely focusing on mail and internet! It was growing close to the new millennium after all, and if anyone should do it – with his computer background and limitless funds – it was him, right?

Getting in a quicker-than-usual workout and rushing home, he gathered a team and launched the business in practically no time at all. He noticed, when he put his mind to something, be it teaching children in Africa or running a company, he was full-force. This new idea, spawned at the gym, was no different.

After preparing the business strategy, Reed felt he had something potentially groundbreaking.

Following a lucrative launch, the website was officially up and running. And as the brand, **which he called Netflix,** became more recognized and users multiplied, Reed knew he was exactly where he needed to be.

The final kingpin on his to-do list was to strike a deal with the powerhouse big-brother, Blockbuster.

Hopping on a plane from Silicon Valley to Dallas in

2000, Reed and his team scheduled an appointment with the culprits of the $40 late fee.

Stepping into the office of Blockbuster's CEO, Reed quickly began explaining his offer. He was willing to sell 49% of Netflix ownership to Blockbuster to act as an online arm for the video-rental giant. Netflix would handle online, Blockbuster would handle in-store. Together, they would team up to serve their customers underneath both brand names.

Ending his spiel with a wide smile, feeling fully confident in his offer, Reed's smile grew sour once he heard the feedback. He didn't receive his 'yes.' Instead – he was practically laughed at. "Um, no, we're fine on our own," was the immediate response.

Nodding his head and thanking Blockbuster for their time, Reed understood he was forced to go at it alone. Yet, he didn't doubt for a second their 'no' would be their loss, not his.

Reed's instincts proved correct, and Netflix, with its adventure-loving, education-focused, forward-thinking leader – found its services utilized in homes across the world. In a matter of five years, Netflix had over 4.5 million subscribers, beating out any online efforts made by Blockbuster.

Ten years later, Netflix even began filming their own shows (such as hit *House of Cards*) and rose their initial stock by almost 10,000%. Today, Netflix is known by nearly everyone in the world, filming original movies and raking in billions annually.

And Reed, the same man who once had no clue where his future would lead, hence became one of the most entrepreneurial extraordinaries of our time.

Holding tightly to his love of movement and adventure, he still captains Netflix today, sprinkling his personality into the workplace — even deciding to forego having his own office so he can instead float around between the desks of his employees.

Reed, worth somewhere in the ballpark of $1.5 billion and known for donating major profits to youth education, truly followed his talent, instincts, and passions, hearing a 'yes' even when the world shouted 'no.'

Back in 1997, Reed recognized something important that day in the gym.

In the 1990's land of Blockbuster, Marky Mark, and video cassettes, the internet was non-existent to the average consumer, so brick-and-mortar movie stores made sense. But with the internet becoming more prominent, Reed anticipated it would change everything — sparking his success with his online masterpiece, Netflix.

Blockbuster lost big when they ignored the Netflix proposal, foregoing futuristic thinking and dismissing the internet's growing market-share. Consequently, **Blockbuster was forced to close its doors and file for bankruptcy in 2010.**

Due to countless horror stories similar to Blockbuster, the power of the internet is no longer ignored, becoming as commonplace as the air we breathe. The internet has become an asset for businesses of all kinds, and only the foolish are overlooking its enormity.

From building an online-based presence to simply advertising online, the internet has become a tool of choice for all major brands.

With the growth of the internet, marketing is now categorized in two forms: online and offline.

And surprisingly enough, online marketing has recently become the top dog for advertising dollars, at 35% of advertising budgets in 2018.

All offline marketing tactics trail behind. TV is at 34%, while radio (9%), magazines (8%), newspapers (8%), billboards (5%), and cinema advertising (3%) are shrinking by the day.

For at least the next few years, the best possible business outcome results from a combination of both online and offline marketing. However, with the youngsters of 'Generation Z' struggling to take their eyes off their WIFI-induced smartphones, it doesn't look like offline marketing will be making much of a comeback in the fight for more advertising dollars anytime soon.

Television is being overtaken by Netflix/Hulu, radio is being overtaken by Pandora/Spotify/Sirius, magazines are becoming obsolete and increasingly expensive, newspapers are going bankrupt right and left, less people see billboards because passengers are on their phones, and there's a reason you don't see any new cinemas being built.

Long story short, online marketing deserves the majority of seats at the table of where to spend marketing capital.

The current main internet arenas include search engine advertising (Google/Bing Ads), social media promotion, organic search engine results, email lists, and re-marketing.

And Google advertising in particular, depending on the industry, should receive more of the budget than all else.

Google is sweeping the world by storm at 70% of searches, as more and more people are using Google for guidance on the who, what, and wheres of life.

When "Where should I..." is typed into Google, the first three recommended searches to pop up are as follows:

– Where should I live?
– Where should I work?
– Where should I go to college?

If people are searching for answers as life-changing as those, it's no shocker they're Googling answers for the smaller questions in life that may include your industry.

With five billion searches a day, Google rules the roost (trailed by Bing, Yahoo, and others at 30% combined), and it's up to both small and large business owners to make sure they've cornered the market in their field, meaning they should be on the first page of their industry in their area.

Google ranks businesses using two priorities: search engine optimization, known as SEO, and search engine marketing, known as SEM.

Search engine optimization, or SEO, refers to the online visibility of a website in Google's <u>unpaid</u> results—often referred to as "natural", "organic", or "earned" results.

Search engine marketing, or SEM, refers to the promotion of website visibility on Google results through <u>paid</u> advertising.

In a nutshell, you don't pay for SEO, you do pay for SEM. Both are crucial, and 99% of uber-successful companies excel using both.

For example, when you type "shoes" into Google, a Zappos.com advertisement pops up right on top (SEM), and they're also the first organic listing underneath the ads (SEO). There's a reason for this: the more money a company invests into

Google Ads, (often) the better their organic listing because they're getting more traffic to their website and therein viewed as more reputable, earning a higher organic spot on the search engine.

SEO, although free, is not always easy. It requires both technical and creative elements in order to improve rankings, drive traffic, and increase awareness in search engines. Some of the tips of SEO include sprinkling 'keywords' (words often Googled by the market in your industry) throughout the verbiage on your website.

When Google views a bakery website, for example, it expects to see 'bakery,' 'cakes,' 'donuts,' 'cookies,' and the like in both the front-end (what the naked eye can read) as well as the back-end (hidden descriptions on websites only computers can read) of the website. If a bakery didn't have a single keyword on their entire website referencing baking, it would be difficult for Google to know they were a bakery at all.

The way to determine the right keywords to use on a website is to figure out what someone would Google to find you. If someone was searching for a bakery or a wedding cake, they would type "wedding cake" or "bakery." And, bingo – those are words to use.

In comparison to SEO, SEM *does* cost money.
Google Ads, the most recognized category of
SEM, requires three main components: budget,
location, keywords.

- The monthly budget determines HOW OFTEN
  the ad will show up at the top of Google.
- The location determines WHERE the
  advertisement will show up.
- The instructed keywords determine WHAT terms
  trigger the advertisement.

The advertisement itself looks just like a normal
Google listing, apart from the small, adjacent "ad"
sticker that often goes unnoticed.

In addition to SEO and SEM, 're-marketing' is
another "Lebron" in the NBA that is online
marketing. Re-marketing, as per the name,
targets individuals whom have previously viewed
the website of your company.

Re-marketing can provide publicity, revenue, and
exposure like no other channel of marketing, and
it's the reason why that same briefcase you
looked at online has been following you for weeks.

Re-marketing starts with placing a special code into the back-end of your business's website.

Once the code is in, the website can track "cookies" and allow advertisements to follow viewers for up to a month after viewing the initial website, working well for organizations with at least 1,000+ views a month on their website.

Instead of advertising to Joe Schmo who has never been on the website before, this type of marketing reels in existing customers (or at least customers who have an interest, hence their previous visit).

Remember, **it costs 7x as much to get a new customer than to retain an existing one**. With a ratio like that, Google cookies may taste better than chocolate chip cookies!

In addition to SEO, SEM, and re-marketing, email distribution is still a player. Although email distribution is becoming saturated, it can still leave a dent.

They say the average consumer views email marketing like they do apps on phones. Most people don't download a new app every day; in fact, most people don't download a new app even once a month! They get their top apps right away and usually stick to the big guys (Spotify, Uber, Instagram, Snapchat, etc).

Email marketing is no different. Other than a few outliers, the average person doesn't sign up and KEEP themselves on email marketing lists on a regular basis. And if they do, they don't read through every email.

The average person has 2–3 companies in which they regularly read the emails describing deals and updates. Obviously, companies are vying to be in that exclusive group.

Email marketing, when created as education instead of screaming "BUY THIS! SHOP NOW!" is the best route to keeping subscribers.

A certain juice shop based in Honolulu ran their email marketing campaign with sweeping success. Each monthly email provided a new smoothie recipe, the first few sentences of the latest healthy–living blog entry on their website (usually related to yoga, travel, or happiness), and a 25% off coupon.

The reason for this particular growing email list is how un–intrusive it is, with subscribers feeling as though they're being educated, not told what to do. It feels more-so like a newsletter or article than an email designed to sell, sell, sell.

The internet is not disappearing. Using SEO, SEM, re-marketing, and email distribution, your company can plan on waving goodbye to the "Blockbusters" of your industry missing the online-boat.

Paige Weslaski

Chapter Ten:

The 'Bieber Fever' Achiever

"God speaks in the silence of the heart."
– Justin Bieber

Knees knelt, head down, and eyes clenched tight, Pattie Mallette continued to pray.

"Lord – Lord God – please provide a bright future for my Jay. Get us out of this low–income housing! Open new doors! Use him like you've never used anyone before. Lord, please."

As a 17–year–old single mother with nothing more than an underpaying office job and a heart to dream, Pattie got up from her knees with a quiet "Amen."

She knew, night after night, the prayers about her newborn were being heard; knowing God would unleash his blessings on Jay so he wouldn't be in a position like her someday. She longed for his life to be special. Rare, even.

As the calendar years fermented, her prayers didn't change. Jay grew into a young boy, and Pattie noticed, slowly, he was different – talented in ways his friends weren't. While he enjoyed sports and games like any other boy his age, he had a peculiar obsession at home: dancing, listening, and singing to all types to music.

Playing the classics in their kitchen, Michael Jackson and Lionel Richie in particular, Pattie noticed how Jay would break out his toddler dance moves. So consequently, when he begged her to begin lessons, she couldn't say no.

Throughout elementary school, while "normal" kids learned one instrument, Jay learned four — piano, drums, guitar, and trumpet. Taking to the instruments beautifully with a voice to match, Jay was becoming known as a 'mini–prodigy' tucked away in his humble Canadian town.

Walking through their quaint downtown square one afternoon, Pattie and Jay stumbled upon a performer playing guitar for tips. Thrilled at the thought, Jay made his plea to do the same; and with a tugged heart, Pattie nodded in compliance.

Thereafter, Jay frequently sang on the downtown sidewalk with a freeway of foot–traffic, growing a crowd.

Beaming while her son sang as confident as if no one was watching, Pattie realized something. Her boy was so different, so unique. THIS was how God would use him… his musical ability!

When Jay entered a local singing contest, her assumption was solidified with a second place win. The next contest, with a bit more practice, he got first.

Pattie felt guilty keeping his talent private, deciding to spread his gift with family and friends using YouTube as the gateway. Singing with the highest of pitches and hardest of notes on a continual basis, Jay grew more talented by the day.

Over time, and with the nature of the internet, his talent soon became no local/family secret. Youtube users all over the nation were mesmerized by his videos, and Jay quickly became the 'most subscribed' artist in all of Canada and 20th in the world, all filmed in his living room.

His big break was right around the corner, and luckily, the young singer didn't have to do a thing. Instead, the break found him.

A marketing executive nicknamed 'Scooter' stumbled on one of Bieber's 2007 videos late at night while searching for another artist. Scooter, mesmerized by Jay singing the enchanting "So Sick" by Neyo, did something unprecedented: he called Jay's school and received the contact info of Pattie, immediately calling and asking if he could sign Jay.

While Scooter convinced the weary Pattie he was no scam, but the real deal, she answered saying she'd think about it.

Pattie, getting on her knees that night and taking the question to God, prayed hard to receive her answer, as she had with so many questions before.

"God, I gave Jay to you, so do what you please. But could you instead send me a Christian executive, a Christian label!? Not this Jewish Scooter guy!"

However, instead of unease, Pattie felt an

overwhelming sense of peace. And when her church family agreed, she knew she had a clear answer: "go."

So, "go" they did. Flying to Atlanta, Scooter wasted no time with the mother–son duo, setting up an audition for Jay with R&B superstar Usher. And luckily, Jay knew just what do sing.

Performing "U Got It Bad," an Usher exclusive, Usher clapped with excitement and a smile. "You're signing with me, kid," he exclaimed with a nod.

Justin Timberlake equally interested in signing the him, Jay, Pattie, and Scooter decided on Usher, and the work began.

Releasing his first song, "One Time," it became a #1 hit. Tween girls went crazy, the media had a frenzy, and YouTube was blown up. **Jay became huge, literally overnight.**

Releasing hit after hit – "One Less Lonely Girl," "Baby," and "Never Say Never," Jay – commonly known as Justin Bieber – swiftly began a tour in major cities around the world, a film crew recording his every move for his theater–based documentary. And the rest, they say, is history.

Ten years ago, Justin and Pattie were average folks with a hidden talent. Today, Justin is one of the most well-known household names in all the world.

"If you don't dream big, there's no use of dreaming. If you don't have faith, there's nothing worth believing," the 24-year-old shares.

Justin's mother started with simply posting a video on social media (i.e. YouTube), and the outcome culminated in her son becoming worth over $225 million. There's something, business-wise, to be learned from that. Social media (clearly) has leverage.

Unlike SEO and SEM discussed in the previous chapter, social media marketing (SMM) is arguably the most important marketing feature in existence. Social media tells a brand's story through a more personal feel than any other form of advertising, allowing the world to get a glimpse of a company's culture.

Marketing expert David Scott put it well: **"You can buy attention (thru advertising). You can beg for attention from the media (thru PR). You can bug people one at a time to get attention (thru sales).**

Or you can earn attention by creating something interesting and valuable and then publishing it online for free."

Social media tells the story of a company better than anything else.

The main social platforms of 2018 are Facebook, Twitter, Instagram, YouTube, Snapchat, LinkedIn, and Pinterest, although it's probable 1+ will be obsolete within the next five years and replaced.

But today, they all matter. A lot. And based on your business and your market, it's likely at least one of those platforms can and should aid your mission.

Each of the platforms is unique in its own way, especially when it comes to the **opportune time of day** for posts. See below:

Facebook: 1 PM to 4 PM
Instagram: 5 PM to 6 PM
Snapchat: 9 PM to 10 PM
Twitter: 1 PM to 3 PM
LinkedIn: 7 AM to 9 AM, 5 PM to 6 PM
Pinterest: 2 PM to 4 PM, 8 PM to 1 AM

And out of all of them, Facebook is the kingpin of

the outlets.

Facebook has the most users by leaps and bounds, even when it comes to millennials (over 76% of youngsters use this platform, versus 43% at 2nd placer Instagram). Facebook covers it all and won't be going anywhere for quite some time.

It's important to note, in 2018, Facebook made an update to how they present businesses. They reformatted their "wall algorithm" so users would see less company posts and more friend posts.

Because of this, even the people who "liked" your Facebook business page will likely not see a whole lot posted.

Due to this update, companies must be more strategic than ever when posting on their Facebook wall. Instead of shouting at Facebook users to "BUY (product/service) NOW!!!," using creative strategies are a better way to get the attention of viewers. And when viewers like what they see, they often choose to click "see first" on friends or companies so they never miss a status.

Some of the ways to become set apart in the social media game are through contests/ giveaways, writing about relevant current events, providing recipes or DIY walk–throughs, using hashtags, humble bragging about company social responsibility, influencer marketing, or imagery.

Since Facebook is the most widely used, Facebook will be the primary platform discussed below (although these tactics can be used on any of the outlets).

CURRENT EVENTS

Tailoring posts based on the **season, weather, or upcoming holidays** makes your page relevant. Here's some light, unbiased examples to post about:

– On Fridays, post about the weekend coming up.
– In late winter, ask viewers what their favorite spring cleaning tips are.
– On Mother's Day, Father's Day, Valentine's Day, etc, create product posts that relate to that theme.

Lowe's understands this principle. In balmy March, they posted a beautiful photo of a manicured lawn surrounding a sleek patio set. The caption read "Dreaming about warmer weather? Our new patio furniture collections can help you start brainstorming!"

Combine current events/seasons/days of the week with your brand. "It's finally Saturday! Stop in tonight between 7–10 for a free beer along with any appetizer!," a bar/grill could post. Make it relevant!

MMM, RECIPES ... OOH, DIY CONTENT

Providing **recipes and DIY walk–throughs** can attract followers.

IKEA does this well. "See how you can combine our bunk beds and children's dressers into a Star Wars fort in this week's DIY video!," they once posted. The post included a link for visitors to click, taking them to the IKEA website to watch. This provided more website clicks (helping their Google ranking) and also drove product sales.

Quest Nutrition, creator of the popular Quest Bars, posts DIY recipe videos regularly. On St. Patrick's Day this year, they created a minute long recipe video with this caption: "We're bringing these Mint Chocolate Chunk PROTEIN Doughnuts to the #StPatricksDay party. Who wants one!?" The video combined mint Quest bars with applesauce, coconut oil, and other ingredients for a yummy treat.

Recipes and DIY walkthroughs, from yummy desserts to installing a desk, provide intel into how to use your product/service in tangible, understandable ways.

#HASHTAG HEAVEN

Since we're on the topic of indulgent treats, let's discuss another splurge–related product: Ben & Jerry's Ice Cream, a master of social media with close to 9 million Facebook fans.

Part of the success behind the Ben & Jerry's success is their use of **#hashtags**.

In one instance, the company wanted to get the word out about their new dairy–free product line, using hashtags to let an entirely new vegan market know they existed. Let me explain… what do you think of when you think Ben & Jerry's? (besides overdoing it on Chunky Monkey when the cheerleading captain denied your prom date request in high school, that is)

Thick, dairy–based ice cream – that's what. But when B&J decided to recreate their wheel and offer something completely out of the box – vegan ice cream – they took to social media to announce it using hashtags.

Ben & Jerry's used their hashtags strategically, along with a photo of a few pints of the product: **"Introducing our #nondairy line in Canada— certified #vegan, made with an almond base, and oh so creamy!"**

With over two billion users on Facebook, many of them must be vegan, and by creating a post that signified their new unveiling, it reeled in an entirely new audience.

Those searching "vegan" or "nondairy" on Facebook via the hashtag feature were then able to see the post and find a new supermarket product to try.

The way hashtags work is that each of them serves as a link to discover content that is all related.

Hashtags are also useful in contest situations. By creating a unique hashtag, any public post or picture with that hashtag can be seen.

For example: "Post a photo of yourself at today's Cubs game with the hashtag #CubsOpeningDay18 for a chance to win a signed baseball!"

Both new and existing hashtags can serve to reel in new customers or grow the brand via existing ones. Create a hashtag for your company that has never been used before, and also be generous with inserting popular hashtags into your posts.

"MOM, I WON!"

Contests and giveaways turn fans into customers.

The difference between a giveaway and a contest is giveaways are usually random, and contests are earned.

A giveaway could be as simple as asking participants to post a picture. For example, if your company is based in LA, you could post a photo of two Los Angeles Rams tickets, posting the status "'Like' our page, tag a friend, and share on your page for a chance to win these tickets!" This grows your following and provides free marketing. Using a service like 'Rafflecopter' makes the contest easy, or you can simply choose a winner by random.

Contests, in contrast, are earned. Home Depot had a Facebook contest asking women to post a bathroom DIY before–and–after photo using a hashtag they had created (#HDDIY2017). Home Depot was going to choose the best renovation and award the winner with a gift card.

Contests and giveaways provide users a game to play, keeping your company worthwhile.

SAVE THE SEALS

Is there any benefit to **philanthropy** besides bettering the world, you ask?

Yep – and the stats prove it. $\frac{2}{3}$ of people say they would pay more for a product or service if the company was socially responsible. For millennials, it spikes to $\frac{3}{4}$!

Philanthropy is not only the moral thing to do, but it will increase sales and well–being amongst the company culture. However, if the good deed isn't shared properly, those benefits vanish. Using social media to "humble brag" about the golf outing sponsorship or computer donation to the local Boys & Girls Club can go a long way for branding.

Dawn Dish Soap jumped on this train. On their social media and television ads, the company has promoted their "Dawn Helps Save Lives" campaign highlighting their involvement aiding birds affected by oil. This promotion always involves a small chick, using the phrase "tough on grease, soft on hands." The philanthropic ploy, along with being incredibly heartfelt, drives sales.

INFLUENCERS

I already know what you're thinking: "I don't know any celebrities!"

The term "influencer" is convoluted and does not just refer to celebrities. An influencer refers to **anyone with general credibility**, whether they be a medical doctor, technology expert, academic, journalist, CEO, board member, or even employee.

Using someone who can boost the credibility of your brand is a wise feature on a social media status or update. But not every influencer works for every company!

An NBA player would be a great influencer for a sports brand or drink, but generally wouldn't make a good fit for the tech industry, for example.

Gatorade used Michael Jordan. Oral B used a dentist. Dior used model Giselle. Keds used Taylor Swift. Viagra used a doctor. Welch's Grape Juice used a five year old.

Every company has a different market and therefore has a different spin on who could work as a valid influencer. Some may even do it for free (...especially if you go the same route as Welch's)!

IMAGE IS EVERYTHING

A picture tells a thousand words, and a video tells a million.

Therefore, it's imperative to be picky with your photos/videos, your 'models,' and even the employees you present on social media. If you own an ice cream parlor, the right person used for an advertisement or post would be a young, college–aged woman with a big smile on her face. If you own a tech company, the right model would be a middle–aged man with a laptop in hand. If you own an assisted living home, the right models would be an elderly couple partaking in some sort of activity, like bingo or bike riding.

If pictures/videos can't be taken, there's free online stock resources available like Pexels.com, Unsplash.com, or Pixabay.com, providing unrestricted pictures and videos.

Image matters, exactly why McDonalds does not use unhappy, disgruntled employees in their social media posts or commercials.

Are You a 'Belieber?'

Bieber once said, "Two people can look at the same thing and see it differently." While one business owner views social media and technology as an unnecessary add-on, another sees it as a vehicle to drive their business into a Narnia of brand-recognition, visibility, and crafted storytelling.

Using current events, DIY content, hashtags, contests, social responsibility tactics, influencers, and captivating imagery, your brand will do nothing but soar.

Don't "unfriend" the idea of social media for your business. It just might get you a metaphorical (or literal) record deal with Usher.

Chapter Eleven:

Bulldogs and Weinermobiles

"I take rejection as someone blowing a bugle in my ear to wake me up and get going, rather than retreat." – Sylvester Stallone

Cars honking their horns and two police sirens competing for ears, the window of a NYC hospital room was overlooking a bustling afternoon. Inside the room, however, life was just as tumultuous.

"Push, honey, push!" the expectant father, Frank, shouted as he squeezed his wife's hand.

"I've never seen something like this before. He really just won't come out," the doctor worried out loud.

"Well, do something! I'm sure you can see this is not enjoyable for her!" Frank exclaimed, an expression mixed of encouragement and rage plastered on his sleep–deprived face.

Grabbing a pair of forceps, the doctor decided he'd have to handle things himself. With a quick prayer for luck, the doctor inserted the tool and managed to secure the baby inside the womb. Slowly, the baby's cries could be heard as he was pulled ever so gently into the world.

In a matter of moments, little Michael was born. But as the nurse handed the baby to Jackie, something seemed off. The baby's lip, tongue, and chin seemed to be bleeding, and Jackie looked back at the nurse.

"The doctor may have slightly nipped the baby with the instrument, but there was no other option," the nurse defended, trying to sound calm as possible.

Looking at her husband, Jackie was nervous this "cut" may have done more damage than they thought.

"He'll get better, Jackie. Won't you – baby Mikey? You're tough." Frank shrugged, who was also secretly worried.

As the nurse cleaned up and the doctor left, there was nothing to do but hope he was right.

The baby grew from infant, toddler, to child, and little Mikey – who everyone called "Sly" – no longer had two married parents like he did upon birth.

The cut on little Michael's face metaphorically foreshadowed the cut between his mother and father, as their relationship had grown more and more tense throughout the pregnancy. The divorce was final shortly after the birth of Sly.

In fact, things grew so shaky, the state of New York intervened, and Sly was placed in the foster system for a few years before returning to his father.

Growing up in the big city with a single dad wasn't easy for little Sly. He was poked fun of for his permanent deformity on his lip, tongue, and chin, all due to the doctor's ignorance. Attending twelve different schools, Sly was kicked out of many of them and had dreadful grades.

A half-paralyzed face and speech impairment, it was difficult to speak to his friends at school without getting picked on. But by the time high school rolled around, Sly had ripened a healthy coping mechanism for his uneasy childhood – drama class, performing in various school plays.

Living in Philly for high school, he finally realized his purpose: to get back to the city and become an actor. One day, he dreamed, no one would laugh at his face again.

Packing up his belongings and English Mastiff pup, Butkus, he moved back, hoping to make it 'big' in the 'Big' Apple.

Without a place to live, however, Sly spent nights sleeping at the bus station, working as many odd jobs as he could scrounge. From cleaning lion cages at the zoo to ushering at the local cinema, Sly was anything but "big." In fact, he felt pretty small.

Finding a room in a flophouse situated above a subway station, he barely scraped by to pay the rent. Butkus the pup, Sly's best friend, even noticed the lack of funds, as his dish became emptier each night.

One afternoon, looking at Butkis with dread in his heart, Sly accepted he wasn't even capable of caring for his pup anymore, barely making ends meet for himself alone. A desperate, empty stomach and eyes welling with tears, Sky walked Butkis down to the nearest 7–11 and sold his best friend for the best price he could find, forty dollars.

Heading back home with a heat of anger and disappointment, Sly felt sick. "Have I grown so low and hungry, I'd sell his only responsibility?" he questioned himself.

Consumed with earning Butkis back, he knew he needed a miracle.

Weeks later, jogging past a sports bar and feeling down as ever, Sly noticed a crowd forming to get inside. Curious, he squeezed his way into the bar to see what everyone was so enamored with.

It was the seventh round of a boxing match on the bar's television, and Muhammad Ali was fighting underdog Chuck Wepner. The commentator on the screen mentioned how Ali was guaranteed a whopping $1.5 million for the match, while Wepner just $100,000.

Wepner was the unlikely contender, yet Sly witnessed as Wepner lasted a full fifteen rounds against Ali, exceeding expectations of everyone.

And it was in that moment, surrounded by a rowdy, drunk crowd, where something within Sly snapped.

That was it. THAT was what Sly needed to make it big, a story! A rags–to–riches, underdog–to–champion story he could sell as a screenplay! If no one would cast him, heck, he'd cast himself!

Sprinting out of the bar, careful not to knock over any beers, Sly ran straight to his flophouse. Glancing at the clock and seeing 11 PM, Sly decided he wouldn't let time get in the way of this idea.

With a pen and paper, Sly sat down and wrote. And wrote. And wrote. Getting up a few times for the sole necessity of using the bathroom, Sly didn't sleep, eat, or think. He wrote.

Twenty hours later, it was finished. Sly held up his masterpiece like fighter Wepner held his arms after lasting fifteen rounds.

These pages, these very pages, would be his ticket to stardom, he convinced himself.

Certain the story was a winner, he went straight to

the top, finding the best movie producers in town. Sending his script, he was soon beckoned for a meeting at a production house.

"$125,000, Sly. Our offer," the producer smiled as he nodded slowly. "It'll be a hit, and with you accepting this check, it'll happen."

Only, Sly knew they wouldn't make it happen, at least not the right way.

Once he mentioned it was a two-for-one deal, that he himself had to be the star, the producer was quick to swap his smile for a frown.

"Look, Sly, you're basically a no-name actor at this point, and you…"

Before the man could finish his argument, Sly was gone.

A few weeks going by without another word, Sly grew nervous, but not nervous enough. Adamant, he knew no starring role meant no movie.

Eventually, getting another ring, he was offered $350,000 for the script alone. Sly again declined; he needed to be the main role! He wrote the script for HIM, and if the company didn't believe in that, they could forget it.

Time ticked, and Sly got one more call. They would take him, he would play the starring role, and they'd use his script. But, he'd get paid just $35,000 total. A no-namer lead meant fewer sales, they reasoned.

Jumping at the chance, Sly rushed to the production house, signed the papers, and scheduled filming.

Euphoric, all his hard work, from sweeping movie theaters to sleepless nights at the train depot, paid off. Only, there was one more piece of business to complete.

Running back to that same 7-11, he searched everywhere for the man who bought Butkis. No luck, he went back the following day. Then the next. Finally, the man showed up, Butkis on a leash next to him.

Seeing his pup, Sly was elated. "Sir, I have the money to care for Butkis. And I want to him back!"

Stubborn as a mule, the man shared he'd grown rather fond of Butkis, too. He wouldn't take the

$100 offered. In fact he wouldn't take $500. Slaphappy, $15,000 was his asking price, and as ridiculous as Sky knew it was, he paid the money, and Butkis was back home.

Launching filming within the year, Sly brought Butkis each day, even scoring him his own role in *Rocky*. "We are NOT hiring another dog to play MY dog!" Sly contended.

Once the film was finished, Sly watched the final product with his director and couldn't believe it. Having poured his heart and soul into the movie, Sly knew his world could and would be turned upside–down with its release.

And his instincts proved correct. Sly – or **Sylvester Stallone** – wrote and starred in *Rocky*, one of the greatest films of all time. He made it, paralyzed face and all. He made it.

Perhaps his *Rocky* character described it perfectly:

"Let me tell you something you already know. The world ain't all sunshine and rainbows. It's a very mean and nasty place and I don't care how tough you are, it will beat you to your knees and keep you there permanently if you let it. You, me,

or nobody is gonna hit as hard as life. But it ain't about how hard ya hit. It's about how hard you can get hit and keep moving forward. How much you can take and keep moving forward. That's how winning is done!"

Sly knew, deep down, that although his script was loosely based off the Wegmer–Ali flight, it was really about him. Sly.

When he thought about it hard enough, he refused to let anyone else play Rocky because **Rocky was Sly.** Sly had gotten beaten down. Sly had faced rejection. Sly had felt unloved and unwanted. But like Rocky, his greatness was there, waiting to be unleashed.

Sylvester Stallone went on to star in dozens of films, including seven more *Rocky* spin–offs, the *Rambo* series, and many others. He was no longer a nobody cleaning the lions den at the zoo, no longer laughed at for his deformity. Instead, he was praised for it.

The production house who filmed *Rocky* had an all–in budget of 1.1 million for the first film, which they held to. This particular budget, since Sly was initially a no–namer and the film's success was questionable, was on target. They really had nothing to lose with that low of a movie budget since it was a gamble.

To their surprise, the film went on to make $225 million, 225x the initial investment. Combined with the other spinoffs, the *Rocky* franchise – to date – has made $677 million dollars, 667x the initial investment. The production house won big.

The problem with most startup companies, however, no matter how unique in nature, is thinking they're the next *Rocky*. Overestimating revenues and underestimating costs, they anticipate an instantaneous strike of gold.

Just reference any *Shark Tank* episode for proof. Of the four or so businesses featured on each episode, at least one uses the argument, "the industry for x, y, z is $500 billion dollars! If we receive just 1% of all '___' consumers, we'll all be BILLIONAIRES!" (insert eye roll)

Everyone thinks "my product/service will be the best, it'll sell out! I need to spend, spend, spend in order to hit the market with a bang!" This mentality, however, drives business owners into a serious black hole of debt, be it via overbuying product in bulk, selling off too much equity, or overspending on marketing in avenues that aren't proven.

On average, startups spend 30% more than initially planned, and revenues are almost always less than anticipated.

You need to spend money to make money, but you don't need to spend as much as your fear is urging you.

"Remember, the mind is your best muscle... big words can move mountains," Sly quotes in *Rocky.*

To his point, with an advantageous product or service, even just hearing via **word of mouth,** people will wait a few extra shipping days while you order more product, drive to an unpopular area of town while you save on overpriced rent, or even donate to a Kickstarter if your idea is catchy enough.

Renting a high–profile building downtown, over-ordering merchandise, over–hiring, or over-spending while making a metaphorical 'questionable movie' (like *Rocky*) can all lead to a company's demise. As confusing as it sounds, **money can cost too much!**

A genius way to gain brand recognition is through

guerrilla marketing. **Guerrilla marketing (not 'hoo-hoo ha-ha' gorilla, mind you), is an advertising strategy for businesses to promote their products or services in an unconventional way with little to no budget.** These tactics are generally as out-of-the-box as it gets.

Guerrilla marketing is an especially wonderful secret for small businesses without money to spend, but also – for BIG businesses WITH money to spend.

One of the most recognizable forms of guerrilla marketing is a giant, moveable hotdog we all know and love: the Oscar Meyer Weinermobile.

Currently, there are six Wienermobiles traveling across the country to festivals, parties, and tailgates, with two Hot Doggers (drivers) per Weiner.

For Oscar Meyer, this investment was a drop-in-the-bucket compared to their massive marketing budget. Investing in the cost of the vehicles, twelve hired hands, and gas, the Weinermobiles are known by hundreds of millions around the country and world as a symbol of goofiness.

That goofiness, however, turns to sales when

customers are standing in the processed meat department choosing their 4th of July party 'dog' of choice. The Weinermobile does its job.

Another large company utilizing guerrilla marketing is Goodyear Tires. Seen at football games, on TV, and major events, the Goodyear blimp is a conversation-starter by anyone happening to see it fly over. The floating publicity for Goodyear Tires has been seen, like the Weinermobile, by an incalculable number, leading to incalculable sales. It worked so well, it's been duplicated considerably.

Dominos Pizza has recently taken an interesting step in the guerrilla game. What was at first seen as just a social media hoax, Dominos started paying municipalities $5,000 to fill each pothole in the city, as long as their logo and tagline "Oh Yes We Did" appeared over the fresh pavement.

Although the logo was just done in spray chalk and didn't last longer than the first rain, the photos themselves served as all Dominos needed, knowing the online world was much bigger than "Nowheresville, Delaware" where few would see the work (nothing personal, Delaware-folk!).

Another fast-food joint we all know and love,

IHOP, employed guerrilla marketing to shine light on their hamburgers. In a marketing hoax via social media, they "changed" their name to IHOB – International House of Burgers. The change went viral, meaning millions now knew IHOP sold burgers. Shortly after the change, the company shared it had all been one big publicity stunt. And it worked.

But one free guerrilla marketing tactic didn't work out so well.

Cell company Vodafone hired two guys to run onto the field of a European rugby game. They wore nothing... except the company's logo via paint across their bodies. The public was so outraged, the CEO issued an apology and donated $30,000 to a local charity for reducing sports injuries. Inappropriate? Very. Effective? Actually, maybe.

Pizza Hut had *not even a "questionable"* guerrilla marketing campaign, but a **legitimate fail**. The pizza palace decided to change their name and logo from the beloved "Pizza Hut" to – "The Hut." The change, which was never a hoax and was actually a legitimate change – was met with gales of laughter from the media and public.

Immediately after the embarrassment, the CEO came out with a confusing press release to try to undo the damage: "Pizza Hut is not changing its name. We are proud of our name and heritage and will continue to be Pizza Hut.... (but) we do use 'The Hut' in some of our marketing efforts," said Brian Niccol, CMO of Pizza Hut.

Although they wanted to broaden their image from just pizzas to salads and pastas, their entire brand rode on the fact they did pizzas. By abandoning the term "pizza," it turned their entire brand into a big question mark. **Papa John's and Domino's laughed into Pizza Hut's dough, literally.**

Apart from mistakes like Pizza Hut's, guerrilla marketing, when done correctly, can be a profitable investment.

From undergarment company Goldtoe putting oversized briefs on statues around New York to Burger King staging an Instagram breakup over a whopper, guerrilla marketing is the new way to "be seen." You'd be amazed what you can live without in the business world.

Guerrilla marketing works for all businesses, small and large. Often, it's very cheap or free, including hanging fliers at the local Starbucks, posting a magnet on your car, creating a Facebook page and inviting friends to like it, writing content for the local newspaper, having a business card drawing at your office, MailChimp email marketing, hosting a free class, giving away balloons/shirts at an event, or lounging around LinkedIn. Are you using guerrilla marketing tactics to promote your company?

Rocky says it all: **"Every champion was once a contender who refused to give up."** Are you going above and beyond to market your business?

Dessert:

Make Today Yours!

As of 2018, it is costing the US government 1.5 cents to make a penny and 7 cents to make a nickel due to rising metal costs. And believe it or not, this translates perfectly to you and me.

Life is one grand acquisition. Based on how we 'spend' our time, business–wise and personal–wise, we get back that which we work toward.

Knowing this, we can question: Are we "overspending" our precious time on a career, focus, or lifestyle we don't deeply love? Is the profit to our happiness minimal? Is our stress outweighing our "well–being earnings?"

What we want in life is out there, ready to find; be it a quieter morning, more productive work day, stronger team, wiser thought–process, new environment, or entirely different habits.

And business aside, the bigger picture comes down to this: **we, friend, are the CEO's of our own lives.** We call the shots, we run the show, we manage the budget, and we hit the 'start' button.

Feeling bogged by monotony or frustrated with a pattern **is on us.** We have more power than we think, and with that power – the power to uplift, upgrade, and even upset – we can change not only our world, but the world of others.

It's foolish to waste our talents on an unhappy life. Because one day, it will end. We'll look back and question: did we live my life — truly live it? We can make that answer 'yes,' today, because God does not promise our tomorrow.

We have the ability to make as big an impact as those featured in this manual. Nice as it would be to get a 'second–chance' after our funeral like the 'appetizer intro' described, we only have one shot. Today's that shot.

With a little over 3,500 Mondays in the average life – they aren't something to dread! Perhaps the late Steve Jobs put it best: **"Remembering you are going to die is the best way to avoid the trap**

of thinking you have something to lose. You are already naked. There is no reason not to follow your heart.”

Imagine if we were granted the opportunity to write our own future obituaries. Would we plan to live void of regrets? Loving our work, family, and life well, using the hands God's given us? Did we achieve our wildest goals and climb the highest mountains?

Our life story – the story we'd dream to tell – is ready to be written.

Although this book may be over, our future is just beginning. **Together, let's use the next few pages to write our hypothetical obituary. And let's do ourselves a favor: let's dream so big, we'd be embarrassed if someone found this book.**

Let's write it big. Let's write it honest. Let's write it – because one day, it just may come true.

MY OBITUARY:

"Always deliver more than expected."

— Larry Page, co-founder of Google

MY OBITUARY:

"Success is not final, failure is not fatal: it is the courage
to continue that counts."

— Winston Churchill

MY OBITUARY:

"If you can't feed a team with two pizzas, it's too large."

— Jeff Bezos, Founder and CEO of Amazon

MY OBITUARY:

"If you are not embarrassed by the first version of your product, you've launched too late."

— Reid Hoffman, co-founder of LinkedIn

MY OBITUARY:

"Always look for the fool in the deal. If you don't find one, it's you."

— Mark Cuban, AXS TV Chairman and entrepreneur

MY OBITUARY:

"Your most unhappy customers are your greatest source of learning."

— Bill Gates, co–founder of Microsoft

MY OBITUARY:

"Wonder what your customer really wants? Ask. Don't tell."

— Lisa Stone, co-founder and CEO of 'BlogHer'

MY OBITUARY:

"The last 10% it takes to launch something takes as much energy as the first 90%."

— Rob Kalin, founder of Etsy

MY OBITUARY:

"Timing, perseverance, and ten years of trying will eventually make you look like an overnight success."

— Biz Stone, co-founder of Twitter

MY OBITUARY:

"Anything that is measured and watched, improves."

— Bob Parsons, founder of GoDaddy

MY OBITUARY:

"Data beats emotions." — Sean Rad, founder of Tinder

MY OBITUARY:

"Don't be cocky. Don't be flashy. There's always someone better." — Tony Hsieh, CEO of Zappos

Paige Weslaski